SONOMA

A FOOD AND WINE LOVERS' JOURNEY

EDITED AND PRODUCED BY

JENNIFER BARRY

PHOTOGRAPHED BY

ROBERT HOLMES

TEXT BY

MIMI LUEBBERMANN

TEN SPEED PRESS

BERKELEY • TORONTO

A Kirsty Melville Book

Ten Speed Press
P.O. Box 7123
Berkeley, California
94707

Distributed in Australia by Simon and Schuster Australia, in Canada by Ten Speed Press Canada,
in New Zealand by Southern Publishers Group, in South Africa by Real Books, in Southeast Asia by Berkeley Books,
and in the United Kingdom and Europe by Airlift Book Company.

Cover and Interior Design: Jennifer Barry Design, Fairfax, CA
Design Production: Kristen Wurz
Project Management: Blake Hallanan
Copy Editor: Carolyn Miller
Proofreader: Linda Bouchard
Indexer: Ken Dellapenta
Map Illustration: Melissa Sweet

Library of Congress Cataloging-in-Publication Data
Barry, Jennifer.
Sonoma : a food and wine lovers' journey / by Jennifer Barry and
Robert Holmes ; text by Mimi Luebbermann ; foreword by John Ash.
p.   cm.
ISBN 1-58008-474-5
1. Cookery. 2. Grocery trade—California—Sonoma County—Guidebooks.
3. Sonoma County (California)—Guidebooks. I. Holmes, Robert. 1943–
II. Luebbermann, Mimi.   III. Title.

TX714.J68   2000
641.59794'18--dc21   2002156521

First printing, 2003

Printed in China
1 2 3 4 5 6 7 8 9 10 – 06 05 04 03

Preceding pages: Looking over Gloria Ferrer Champagne grapevines, Carneros District *(page 1)*. Redwoods edge Russian River Valley–appellation
vineyards *(pages 2–3)*. Fall colors in Iron Horse Vineyards, Sebastopol *(pages 4–5)*. Holstein dairy cows grazing between milkings *(pages 6–7)*.
Loaves of fresh bread left to rise, Della Fattoria, Petaluma *(pages 8–9)*. Larry Peters holds two wheels of his handmade cow's milk cheese, Spring Hill
Cheese, Petaluma *(pages 10–11)*. Just-picked plum and cherry tomatoes, Healdsburg farmers' market *(pages 12–13)*. Old French oak
fermentation tanks formerly used in an Alexander Valley winery *(pages 14–15)*. Wine grapes ripe for picking *(page 16)*.

FOREWORD

I first experienced Sonoma County when I moved to San Francisco after graduating from college in the late '60's. Then Sonoma was pretty rural—"hicksville" as one of my city friends called it. My first memory of any kind of agricultural act was driving north across the Golden Gate Bridge to a Christmas tree farm in Sonoma to bring back a freshly cut tree lashed to the top of my car. Quite an adventure—not having been a boy scout I lost the tree on the highway because I was and still am "knot challenged."

Next to the tree farm, however, was a small farm stand that was selling all kinds of harvest foods including dried beans; hard winter squash; the last of the apples, pears, walnuts; and the most amazing collection of wild mushrooms that I had ever seen. There was nothing like this available in supermarkets at that time. It was a life-altering discovery for me. The recollection of that stand and those amazing products is as clear for me today as it was then. I was hooked! That Sonoma farm stand was the catalyst for me to make the trip north whenever I could to dig out and discover the other treasures of this magical part of the world. Wine was just beginning to make its mark on the landscape. Apple, pear, prune, plum, and walnut orchards existed here for a long time along with dairies, poultry, and fishing.

I felt possessed—I had to live there. Haven't we all felt that way at least once in our lives? The thought of having all these amazing products right in my back yard was a cook's dream. I was lucky enough to do my early culinary training in France and that set a standard for the importance of using food that was, as much as possible, seasonal, local, and wholesomely grown. The palate was right here.

I opened up my namesake restaurant, John Ash & Company, in Santa Rosa in 1980 and the adventure began. As wine took on more importance, it brought national and then international attention to Sonoma County. An important publication at the time called Sonoma "America's Provence" because of the unique diversity and richness of its agriculture. That seemed to be one of those pivotal moments that acted as the catalyst for more agricultural and culinary diversity. I remember meeting Laura Chenel (the godmother of goat cheese in America) around that time. She had just started making cheese and I can still picture her bringing some of those first cheeses to the back door of the restaurant. Goat cheese had not yet become a part of most of American's palate but we persevered. Times are certainly different, aren't they? Today we acknowledge Sonoma as a leader in changing not only California's but the nation's sense of what good and real food is!

The authors of this book have captured so much in this volume. Not only the beauty of this special place but a deeper connection to the colorful souls that make such a difference here. No matter where we live, the choices made about the food we eat and the wine we drink are ultimately the most profound connection to the world around us. The appreciation that we have for those who provide us with sustenance is a demonstration of the sacred community that I think most of us yearn for. This is a book that I hope you'll return to often both to use the recipes and to be reminded of the pleasure that comes from real food and wine, grown with love, respect, and joy. We need to be reminded, as Wendell Berry suggests, that in the pleasure of food we experience and celebrate our dependence and our gratitude, for we are living from mystery, from living things we did not make and powers we cannot comprehend—the sacred community around us all.

—John Ash, Sonoma County, 2002

Left: A picnic lunch at Buena Vista Winery, Sonoma Valley

INTRODUCTION

For all its average size, 1,579 square miles, Sonoma County surprises in its astonishing variety of geography, topography, landscape, and climate. Beginning on its western border, with the Pacific Ocean splashing on seventy-six miles of rocky cliffs and sandy beaches, the county rolls eastward up coastal mountains clothed with dense forests of redwoods and ferns, then inland to gently inclining grassy hills and valleys patched with deciduous and evergreen oaks, fragrant bay trees, madrone, and manzanita, until the Mayacamas Mountains rise up as the demarcation line between the Sonoma and Napa Valleys. Along the way, eucalyptus groves planted in the early 1900s spice the air with their medicinal scent, marking property boundaries and lining small country roads. Falling-down rock walls, borderlines for pastures or property lines, often date back to the time of the original landowners, when hired help (Native Americans, Chinese, or Latino workers) cleared rocky fields while making barriers for livestock.

The Pacific Ocean's watery bulk tempers the winter cold and blows in cleansing high-flying afternoon fog during the rainless summer months. Rainfall starts in October, and if the farmers are lucky, it ends with a gentle spring rain in May, late enough to keep the grass growing for livestock production but not so late as to disturb the flower set of the wine grapes. Without rain, the bright green hills gradually fade to a luminous gold from June until the late fall rains renew the grass again.

The topography of the county creates multiple climate zones. Redwood trees, growing up to 360 feet tall, soak up the coastal moisture spilling off the ocean along the Sonoma coast. The summer fog churns through the gaps in the coastal range, blasting in a humid coolness beneficial to both plants and animals during the long dry season. Thus the range both funnels and impedes the fog, creating myriad microclimates. At higher elevations above the fog line, warm patches exist, while below the line are pockets where icy cold air slides down to the inland valleys. Consequently, in this small area an astonishing variety of crops and animals thrives from hill to hill, valley to valley. Pinot Noir, Chardonnay, and Champagne grapes revel in the cool fog-laden zones, while Cabernet Sauvignon grapes soak up the valley heat. Sheep and dairy cows thrive in the dewy pastures close to the coast, while the ducks and chickens do better in the slightly warmer, less damp areas farther inland.

For thousands of years, the original residents of Sonoma County, the Coast Miwok, Pomo, and Wappo tribes, lived off the richness of the land. Clams, abalones, mussels, seaweed, and sea urchins were harvested from the ocean's shore. Salmon that migrated up the streams to spawn were trapped, and king salmon were speared in the bays. The bear and deer that lived in the thickets on the slopes of the hills were hunted with bow and arrow. Tanbark, valley oak, coast live oak, and black oak acorns were ground into flour that, when washed in tightly woven willow baskets, lost its bitter bite and was made into gruel or a cakelike bread. The native tribes lived well until their paradise was lost due to the influx of Europeans.

The first European settlers came down from the north. The Russians arrived in Sonoma County in 1812, moving south down the West Coast from Alaska, eager to trap the sea otter, whose luxuriously thick, glossy pelts made fortunes in Russia. They built a stockade, which they named Fort Ross, on the coast above the mouth of the Russian River. A self-sufficient community, Fort Ross became a busy international trading post until the sea otter was hunted almost to extinction in the 1830s. Although the Russians established ranches farther inland in an attempt to balance their loss of otter skin revenue with agricultural income, the settlement was ordered abandoned in 1839 and offered up for sale.

Other visitors to Sonoma County came from the south. Starting in 1769, the Spanish missionaries began working their way up the California coast from Mexico, opening missions roughly a day's horse ride apart. Sonoma County became the convivial meeting place between the Russians at Fort Ross on the coast and the Spanish at the Mission San Francisco Solano, established in Sonoma in 1823. The agricultural heritage of both these cultures is still evident in the county today, from Gravenstein apples (reputedly first introduced at Fort Ross by one of the international travelers), to the grapevines planted by the Russians in 1817 and the Spaniards soon thereafter. After Mexico seceded from Spain, General Mariano Guadalupe Vallejo was granted the Sonoma mission in 1834, and he added to the original grapevines and began to bottle a red wine poetically called Lachryma Montis, or Tear of the Mountains, after the spring on his property.

Wine has continued to be an integral part of Sonoma County's agricultural heritage. The myriad microclimates provide numerous wine appellations for Sonoma County vintage wines, as well as sub-appellations, more than the even-climated Napa Valley or any other California wine region. Appellations are geographical areas designated an American Viticultural Area by the Bureau of Alcohol, Tobacco, and Firearms.

The Sonoma Coast appellation begins in Petaluma, the southernmost town in the county, and heads west to the ocean and north up the coast to include recently planted coastal vineyards. The meandering Russian River, a pathway for Pacific marine air streaming in toward the riverside vineyards, creates the Russian River Valley appellation. Green Valley, Chalk Hill, and a part of Alexander Valley all are affected by the cool hand of the fog and are included as sub-appellations in the Russian River Valley appellation.

Similarly cooled by fog winds, but in an area just off the San Pablo Bay, the Carneros/Sonoma appellation is renowned for Pinot Noir, Chardonnay, and sparkling wine grapes. The Sonoma Valley appellation is located some thirty miles from the coast and is shut off from coastal influence by Sonoma Mountain, so that the temperatures rise up in the daytime and lower only moderately at night. Sonoma Mountain itself is a smaller sub-appellation of Sonoma Valley. The Alexander Valley, a hot interior valley contained between mountain regions, produces rich wines from grapes that luxuriate in hot weather, as do those of another interior valley just to the west, the Dry Creek Valley. Knights Valley, the most easterly wine-growing appellation of northern Sonoma, has the hottest day- and nighttime temperatures.

The county boasts a wealth of agricultural families who trace their ancestry to settlers arriving in the county during the nineteenth century. These families still bring crops to market, along with ex-urbanites who fled cities to become gardeners and farmers. The agricultural community comes together yearly to celebrate in local county fairs, with children in 4-H and Future Farmers of America showing the animals they have raised, weekly local farmer's markets, and county-wide culinary events that draw audiences from the entire San Francisco Bay area. The Gravenstein Apple Fair held

in August has been an ongoing event since 1910. Annual culinary events, such as the Grapes to Glass wine celebration featuring the Russian River Appellation wineries and the Labor Day weekend Sonoma County Wine Auction, are all capped by the October Harvest Fair, highlighting wine and Sonoma County products.

The agricultural families in Sonoma County have had to weather market changes in their crops, from the rise and fall of the hops that fueled the early breweries, to eggs and chickens, which propelled many Petaluma families into prosperity, to prunes and apples, many of which have been replanted today with wine grapes, a crop now bringing higher prices per ton. As the markets fluctuate and change, the farmers, agile and resilient, learn to rethink, to replant, and to take advantage of new opportunities. Sonoma County's proximity to the San Francisco Bay area allowed nineteenth-century farmers to send eggs, milk, cream, meat, vegetables, hops, and cheese first on wind-propelled boats, then on steamers to feed the Forty-Niners during the Gold Rush. Now, in the twenty-first century, farmers continue to raise crops to feed local residents as well as those in the whole San Francisco region and to send to restaurants across the nation.

The fertility of the soil, the friendliness of the mild climate, and the dedication of the farmers—from the old families to new arrivals—have raised the county's agricultural standard of excellence to a level recognized the world over. The county produces food with great abandon whether it be award-winning olive oils, internationally recognized wines, fragrant cheeses, chewy country breads, or herbed pork sausages, to more earthly pleasures such as melons, heirloom tomatoes, and fresh garden greens. Food and travel magazine editors regularly arrive in the county for culinary treasure hunts, from orchards to wineries to dairies, and then to the restaurants that so enthusiastically showcase local farm products. For the seasoned gourmet, wandering tourist, or contented resident, savoring the bright taste of freshly harvested produce, sipping superb wines, locally brewed beers or apple ciders, while savoring local cheeses, the astonishing supply of food produced by the county's sophisticated agriculturalists can make them believe they have fantastically turned onto a road in Provence or Tuscany. Yet, as most local residents will proclaim, often smugly, "it's just Sonoma County."

—Mimi Luebbermann

SOUTHERN SONOMA

SOUTHERN SONOMA

The town of Petaluma, at the headwaters of the Petaluma River, is the second largest in southern Sonoma County, after Santa Rosa, the county seat. The Petaluma River is a tidewater stream, dependent on the ebb and flow of San Pablo Bay, which, in its turn, is the northern edge of the San Francisco Bay. At low tide the river is muddy and sluggish, but before dikes sealed in much of it and infill clogged its channels, Petaluma was a busy commercial port. Shipping food products down the river made tidy fortunes for Sonoma County farmers. A steamer could sail to Petaluma from San Francisco in just five hours.

Petaluma hatched a chicken and egg industry in the first years of the twentieth century when one of its residents, Lyman Byce, invented the egg incubator, allowing the raising of thousands and thousands of chickens to produce millions and millions of eggs, a feat impossible before mechanization. The process of waiting for chickens to become broody in the spring and maybe in the fall and then, if lucky, successful in hatching a dozen or so eggs at a time, could never have allowed such an industry to develop.

By 1917, Petaluma had become nationally known as "The Egg Basket of the Western World." Cooled by the Petaluma Gap, a break in the coastal range that allows the inflow of summer fog, chickens thrived, as did milk cows and market gardeners. County farmers loaded their products onto steamers and sent them down to San Francisco. So much money was made from these enterprises that wealthy Petaluma residents imported Bay Area architects such as Brainerd Jones and Julia Morgan, the architect of Hearst Castle, to build their houses. By a fluke of geology, Petaluma's historic architecture was spared in the terrible earthquake of 1906, so these houses still exist, while Santa Rosa's historic district was totally destroyed.

Today, Petaluma is the eastern starting point for coastal wineries, while just over Sonoma's southern county border McEvoy Ranch produces certified organic extra virgin olive oil from some eighteen thousand trees. Petaluma Processors, the first certified organic chicken producer in America, maintains the city's poultry tradition along with a number of egg producers.

Cow dairies, as well as sheep and goat dairies, still thrive here thanks to the damp coastal air that leaves the pastures green longer in spring and keeps the animals cooler in summer. Clover-Stornetta Farms is one of the local cow dairies owned by a group of dairymen and headed by Dan Benedetti, whose grandparents arrived in Sonoma in 1913 from Tuscany to establish a dairy.

For its conventionally produced milk, Clover-Stornetta sets high standards, contracting with fifteen dairies for milk that is bovine-growth-hormone free. Their organic milk comes from local dairies such as St. Anthony Farm, the first organic dairy in the county. Clover-Stornetta is a beloved business due in part to its figurehead, Clo the Cow, who has become the subject of an amusing advertising campaign seen on billboards throughout the county.

Along the coast, on the edge of Marin County, lie the oyster farms of Tomales Bay, a long inlet refreshed by the circulating water of the Pacific. The continually cold ocean water allows farmed oysters, clams, and mussels to be harvested year-round, much to the joy of locals and visitors, as well as fine restaurants from coast to coast.

To the northeast, at the southern edge of the Sonoma Valley, lies the Carneros appellation, where Sonoma Creek threads its way through vineyards to San Pablo Bay. With winds blowing in cooling air most late-summer afternoons, the climate is perfect for growing Chardonnay and Pinot Noir grapes, and is agreeable to Laura Chenel's goats, which frolic in pastures that were once home to the cows of the locally renowned Stornetta Dairy.

Left: Holstein dairy cows graze on gently rolling hills scattered with deciduous oak trees. The creek beds, dry in summer, become roaring torrents dividing up pastures during the rainy season.
Above: Buyers at the San Francisco farmers' market sample Sonoma County cheese. City dwellers have the opportunity to learn firsthand from Sonoma farmers where their food comes from and to appreciate the long hours of labor involved.

Left: Jim Kehoe, in charge of the dairy at St. Anthony Farm, sets up the stainless-steel milking tank for the next milking of the herd of 240 Holstein cows. The herd is milked twice daily, producing eighteen hundred gallons of certified organic milk every day. The milk travels straight from the cow to the tank through pipes to ensure perfectly clean and wholesome milk.

Top: Some Sonoma barns, made with hand-hewn redwood planks and corrugated tin roofs, may date back to the 1900s or even earlier. The tight grain of the redwood makes the wood long lasting, even when exposed to the elements. Hand-cut redwood fence posts from the last century can still be seen set between metal posts, and they often outlive manufactured material, even though buried in the soil.

Above: Distinctive black and white patterns mark Holstein cows. Among the largest of cows, Holsteins produce great quantities of milk, an average of six to seven gallons each milking. Most dairies, whether of goats, sheep, or cows, milk twice daily, although some cow dairies milk three times a day.

Top: Animals grazing on Sonoma County's grasslands produce prodigious amounts of milk products. Clo the Cow represents Clover-Stornetta Farms, a locally owned company run by a group of dairymen who set strict guidelines for their member dairies, including the prohibition of bovine growth hormone, used by some dairies to artificially increase milk production.

Above: Redwood Hill Farm goat dairy produces award-winning cheeses. Jennifer Bice and her late husband, Steven Schack, took over her parents' goat dairy in 1978. Her Camembert-like Camellia and other aged goat cheeses, as well as her yogurt and fresh cheeses, are sold both locally and nationally.

Right: Goats graze on a hillside in Chileno Valley, Petaluma. Winter and spring rains keep the grass green from November to June. Sonoma County's fog-cooled summer temperatures increase the milk production in dairy animals.

LAURA CHENEL'S CHEVRE

Laura Chenel loves her goats. Growing up in Sebastopol, she raised goats as a hobby and then began what would be her lifelong quest: to find a way to use the milk they produced. Now, some thirty years later, she still puts the goats first and the cheese making second, as a necessary adjunct to their milk production. Even though there are almost four hundred goats at the dairy, every one has a name badge hanging around its neck, and as Laura walks through the barns with a visitor she calls out their names and describes their last kidding, or their place in the milking order.

Laura wasn't satisfied with her beginning cheese-making efforts. With the determination that makes her a premier cheese maker today, she moved to France in 1979 to apprentice at four different goat cheese cooperatives, each with centuries of experience in making fine cheese. She returned home to Sonoma County and began making her own French-style cheeses. When Alice Waters tasted one, she ordered immediately. At her restaurant, Chez Panisse, Alice created a signature dish still served there today: warmed rounds of Laura Chenel's chevre covered in bread crumbs, baked, and served on a bed of tossed mixed salad greens. This dish became a classic of early California cuisine, and the taste for goat cheese began to spread from the restaurant chef to the family shopper.

Today, with the myriad of domestic and foreign goat cheeses offered in specialty cheese shops and sold in national supermarkets, a neophyte might find it hard to believe that just twenty years ago goat cheese was a rarity in America. It is hard not to draw the conclusion that it was Laura Chenel who changed all that. She not only made cheese, she wrote books about it, and she spent countless days handing out samples at national culinary shows, supermarkets, bookstores, and wherever else she could find an audience.

In 1993, she moved her dairy and cheese factory from Santa Rosa to the old Stornetta Dairy, long a landmark for travelers on the busy road

from Sonoma to Napa. The dairy, perched on the edge of a hill, is gleaming white, with a corrugated tin roof. The quiet outside is misleading, for in the back of the dairy, goats are everywhere, feeding at mangers or nibbling visitors' clothes.

The goats are milked twice a day, spending the time in between milkings out in the pastures. Each one is carefully tracked for its milking record, health, and kidding history. Laura supervises the breeding program, so that careful selection improves her herd. Students come regularly from the U.C. Davis veterinary program for hands-on work with the goats. Her dairy staff is chosen for its skill at working with the animals. Her milkers work kindly and gently, which she feels contributes to her herd's excellent milk production.

She feels the same about her staff in the cheese factory, for most have been with her for more than five years. Laura's goal is to turn out a consistent, high-quality product, and that starts with the milk and continues with excellent staffing and impeccable cleanliness in the cheese factory. Visitors don laboratory coats and hair-nets, and must walk through chlorine foot baths. As a sign of her long business association with her customers, Laura produces her cheese on demand, supplying orders with no cheese left over. Although the dairy milks about 350 goats and collects milk from eleven other family farms with about two hundred goats each, the factory is at maximum capacity for the amount of milk available. Even though Laura has some plans for new cheeses, she feels she has found a balance in her business.

As for now, the cheese factory turns out seven different cheeses, some herb or pepper flavored, and one, the cabecou, is marinated with olive oil and herbs in a glass jar. The fresh cheeses, like the chabis, the log, and the fromage blanc, are packaged immediately, while the aged cheeses—the crottin, the taupiniere, and the tome—take weeks or months to ripen.

Leaving the barns after leading a tour, Laura takes off her black rubber boots, changing back into clean white sneakers. She muses that as an old lady, retired from cheese making, she expects she will still be surrounded by goats. And eating cheese, one presumes.

Left and above: Laura Chenel started the goat cheese revolution in California when she came back from a cheese apprenticeship in France and began making goat cheese in Sonoma County in the early 1980s. Chenel maintains the fondness for her goats that began when she first raised goats as a teenager. Her affection for her animals leads her to choose and train her barn and milking staff carefully, and to maintain the highest standards of feed and medical care.

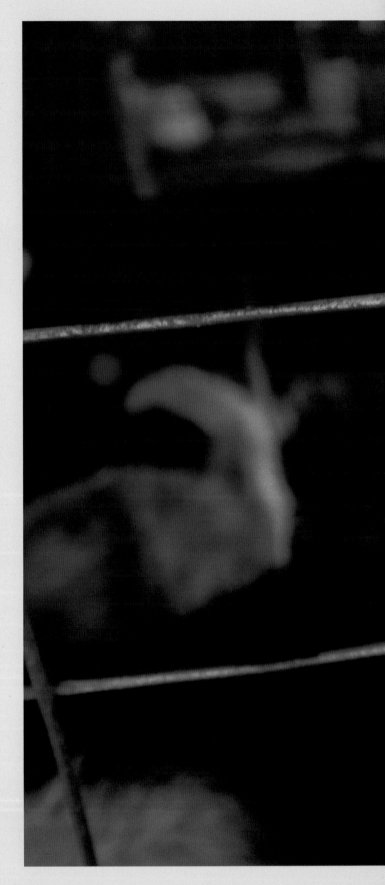

Top, above, and right: Goats come in from their loafing area to receive a portion of grain while they are milked. The milkers work gently with the animals, taking time to note symptoms of illness or anxiety that might lessen milk production. Young goats need patient training to become steady milkers. Laura feels her high milk production results from the attention paid to each animal. The friendly and beguiling nature of goats makes them beloved farm animals, whether in backyards with 4-H members, on small family farms, or in larger commercial dairies.

Laura buys milk from a number of small goat dairies for her cheeses. She makes fresh cheeses, ready to eat, and aged cheeses, which she holds at special temperature and humidity levels to develop their rich, full-bodied flavors. Aged cheeses have a drier texture than the moist, creamy fresh cheeses.

Left, top, and above: Petaluma Farms is owned and operated by Steve Mahrt, a third-generation poultry producer. He began raising chickens in 1983, but he couldn't afford the standard small cages for his chickens, so he allowed them to roam around the barns, free-range by necessity. Still producing eggs from free-range chickens today, Petaluma Farms produces fertile, organic, and conventional eggs, although all his flocks are antibiotic free. Additionally, convinced by medical studies that they are healthier for his customers, he has begun producing omega-3 eggs.

Grilled Fig and Goat Cheese Salad

The Girl & the Fig, Sonoma

This signature salad highlights the first fresh figs of the season. —*John Toulze, executive chef*

2 ounces pancetta, diced
8 fresh black Mission or Turkey figs,
   halved lengthwise (see note)
4 bunches baby arugula
1 cup pecan halves, toasted
¾ cup (4 ounces) crumbled Laura Chenel goat
   cheese
Freshly ground pepper
Fig and Port Vinaigrette (recipe follows)

In a large sauté pan or skillet, sauté the pancetta over medium heat until crisp. Using a slotted spoon, transfer to paper towels to drain. Brush the figs with the pancetta fat from the pan.

Heat a grill pan over high heat and grill the figs for about 45 seconds on each side.

In a stainless-steel bowl, combine the arugula, pecans, pancetta, and goat cheese. Add ¾ cup of the vinaigrette and toss to coat.

Divide the salad mixture among 4 chilled plates and surround with the grilled figs. Grind pepper over the salad and serve. *Serves 4 as a first course*

Note: If fresh figs aren't in season, substitute good-quality moist dried figs. Don't grill them—just cut them into small pieces and toss with the other salad ingredients. Refrigerate any leftover vinaigrette for up to 3 months and use to marinate chicken or pork.

Wine-pairing suggestion: 2000 La Crema Viognier

Fig and Port Vinaigrette

10 dried black Mission figs
3½ cups ruby port
1 cup red wine vinegar
1 tablespoon minced shallots
1¾ cups canola oil blended with ¾ cup
   olive oil
1 teaspoon salt
½ teaspoon freshly ground pepper

Soak the figs in ½ cup of the port for 2 hours, or until soft. In a saucepan, cook the remaining 3 cups port over medium heat to reduce by half. In a food processor, purée the figs, soaking port, reduced port, and vinegar. Add the shallots. Gradually whisk in the oil. Add the salt and pepper. Use now, or refrigerate for up to 3 months. Use for a variety of salads and to marinate chicken and pork. *Makes about 5 cups*

Fava Bean Salad

Bodega Goat Cheese, Bodega

This salad is made with our queso fresco, a fresh white cheese also known as the "goat cheese of the Andes."
It is similar to a young feta because it has never been submerged in salt brine. It's great on salads and melts over pasta
or pizza. Also try it sliced thin in sandwiches or melted in quesadillas. —Patti Karlin, owner

2 pounds young fava beans, shelled

8 ounces queso fresco, preferably from
  Bodega Goat Cheese, crumbled

2 cups cooked corn kernels

2 potatoes, cooked and finely chopped

1 red bell pepper, seeded, deribbed,
  and cut into thin slices

1 large carrot, peeled and shredded

1 Bermuda onion, thinly sliced

Dressing

¼ cup canola oil

Juice of 1 lemon or lime

Salt, cayenne pepper, and freshly ground pepper

1 pound salad greens

❧ Blanch the fava beans in salted boiling water for 2 minutes. Drain and plunge into ice water to cool. Drain again. Pinch the edge of each bean and slip off the skin. In a large bowl, combine the favas, cheese, and the other vegetables.

❧ For the dressing, whisk the oil and juice together in a small bowl. Whisk in the salt, cayenne, and pepper to taste. Divide the greens among 8 salad plates and top with the fava mixture. Pour the dressing over the salad and serve. *Serves 8 as a first course*

Wine-pairing suggestion: Wild Hog Pinot Noir

Goat Cheese Soufflés

St. Francis Winery Kitchen, Santa Rosa

A delicious and sophisticated first course or light lunch with a salad that works surprisingly well
with a light to medium red wine such as Merlot. —Todd Muir, chef

Unsalted butter for soufflé cups, plus 2 tablespoons

Dried bread crumbs for soufflé cups

2 tablespoons flour

1 cup milk

1 teaspoon minced garlic

½ teaspoon herbes de Provence

4 eggs, separated

½ cup aged goat cheese, crumbled

Pinch of salt

Freshly ground pepper

❧ Preheat the oven to 400°F. Butter six 5-ounce soufflé cups and coat the inside with bread crumbs. In a heavy, medium saucepan, melt the 2 tablespoons butter over low heat. Add the flour and cook for 3 to 4 minutes, stirring constantly. Gradually whisk in the milk. Bring to a boil over medium heat. Add the garlic and herbes de Provence. Remove from heat and let cool slightly.

❧ Beat the egg yolks lightly and add to the milk mixture with the goat cheese and salt. Add pepper to taste. In a large bowl, beat the egg whites until soft peaks form. Gently fold the egg whites into the goat cheese mixture. Fill each soufflé cup about three-fourths full with the soufflé mixture. Bake on the center rack of the oven for 15 minutes, or until the soufflés have risen nicely and have a light golden color. Serve at once. *Makes 6 individual soufflés; serves 6 as a first course*

Wine-pairing suggestion: 1999 St. Francis Sonoma County Merlot

Baby Spinach Salad with Warm Sonoma Goat Cheese

The Duck Club Restaurant, Bodega Bay Lodge and Spa

I like this recipe because of the balance of the creamy goat cheese and the sweetness of the oranges and cherries, mixed with the spinach leaves. —Jeffrey Reilly, executive chef

Goat Cheese Cakes

1 cup panko (Japanese bread crumbs), toasted
⅓ cup almonds, toasted and ground
½ bunch chives, minced
Six 2-ounce medallions chilled Laura Chenel goat cheese
1 egg beaten with ¼ cup water

Orange-Sherry Vinaigrette

¾ cup olive oil
⅓ cup aged sherry vinegar
¼ cup frozen orange juice concentrate, thawed
2 shallots, finely diced
3 tablespoons chopped fresh tarragon
Salt and freshly ground pepper

¾ cup dried tart Michigan cherries
1 cup port wine
9 cups baby spinach leaves
3 oranges, peeled and cut into segments
½ cup sliced blanched almonds, lightly toasted

For the cakes, preheat the oven to 350°F. In a bowl, combine the panko, almonds, and chives. Stir to blend. Dip each medallion in the egg mixture, then the panko mixture, coating evenly. Place on a baking sheet lined with parchment paper and bake for 8 minutes.

Meanwhile, make the vinaigrette: In a small bowl, whisk all the ingredients except the salt and pepper together. Add salt and pepper to taste.

Put the dried cherries in a nonreactive saucepan, add the port, and heat over low heat for 4 to 5 minutes, or until the cherries absorb the port.

In a large bowl, toss the baby spinach with the vinaigrette. Divide among 6 salad plates and top with the oranges, cherries, and almonds. Put a warm goat cheese medallion on top of each serving, and you're in luck. You've made one sweet salad! *Serves 6 as a first course*

Wine-pairing suggestion: Ferrari-Carano Chardonnay

Crane Melon Sorbet

Crane Melons, Penngrove

This is a refreshing summer dessert. We like to serve it with fresh melon slices on the side, garnished with a sprig of mint. —Cindi and Jennifer Crane

One 5–6 pound Crane melon, peeled, seeded, and chopped in large chunks, reserving 12 small slices for garnish
1 cup spring water
½ cup sugar
1 tablespoon fresh lime or lemon juice
Fresh mint sprigs for garnish

Place the melon in a blender or food processor and process until smooth. Reserve 3½ cups pureé in the blender, discarding the rest. Combine the pureé with all the remaining ingredients, and process again until smooth. Refrigerate for at least 2 hours, or until thoroughly chilled.

Transfer to an ice-cream maker and freeze according to the manufacturer's instructions. Serve scoops of sorbet in shallow bowls and garnish with reserved melon slices and a sprig of mint. *Makes 1 quart; serves 6 as a dessert*

GRILLED LAMB T-BONES WITH LAURA CHENEL GOAT CHEESE GNOCCHI AND PEPERONATA

Zazu, Santa Rosa

This dish combines two of our favorite Sonoma County products. The goat cheese gnocchi are a twist on traditional ricotta gnocchi. The colors on the plate are gorgeous. We serve broccoli rabe alongside this dish.
—Duskie Estes and John Stewart, chef-owners

Gnocchi

1 pound Laura Chenel goat cheese at room
    temperature
2 eggs
Kosher salt and freshly ground pepper
¾ cup plus 1 tablespoon all-purpose flour

Peperonata

2 tablespoons olive oil
2 cloves garlic, minced
½ yellow onion, cut into ½-inch-thick slices
1 red bell pepper, seeded, deribbed, and cut into
    ½-inch-thick slices
1 yellow bell pepper, seeded, deribbed, and cut
    into ½-inch-thick slices
1 poblano chile, seeded, deribbed, and cut into
    ½-inch-thick slices
Kosher salt and freshly ground pepper

Eight 2-inch-thick lamb T-bone steaks
Olive oil for coating
Kosher salt and freshly ground pepper
1 tablespoon fennel seed, ground in a spice mill

Sauce

2 tablespoons olive oil
3 cloves garlic, thinly sliced
¾ cup dry red wine
¾ cup heavy whipping cream
2 red bell peppers, roasted, peeled, and puréed
    in a food processor
1 teaspoon chopped fresh marjoram
Kosher salt and freshly ground pepper

Mint Salad

Leaves from 2 mint sprigs
2 green onions, including green parts, cut into
    thin diagonal slices
Leaves from 2 flat-leaf parsley sprigs
1 teaspoon extra virgin olive oil
1 lemon wedge
Kosher salt and freshly ground pepper

Prepare a fire in a charcoal grill or preheat a gas grill to medium. The steaks can also be seared on the stove top and finished in the oven if you prefer. Or, use a grill pan.

To make the gnocchi, combine the goat cheese, eggs, and a pinch of salt and pepper in a bowl. Beat until combined. Stir in the flour just until blended. Turn the dough out onto a lightly floured surface and flatten it into a disk 1 inch thick. Using a large knife, cut it into strips 1 inch wide. Roll each strip on the surface to round the edges and cut into pieces about 1 inch long. Place on a baking sheet sprinkled with flour and set aside, or refrigerate for up to 1 day covered with parchment paper.

For the peperonata, heat the oil in a sauté pan or skillet over medium heat. Add the garlic and sauté until fragrant, about 1 minute. Add the onion and sauté for about 5 minutes, or until translucent. Add the bell peppers and chile and sauté until soft, about 10 minutes. Season with salt and pepper to taste.

Meanwhile, make the sauce for the gnocchi: Heat the oil in a sauté pan or skillet over high heat and sauté the sliced garlic until fragrant, about 1 minute. Add the wine and cook to reduce by half. Add the cream and cook to reduce by half. Stir in the pepper purée, marjoram, and salt and pepper to taste. Keep warm in pan.

Coat the lamb with olive oil and sprinkle with salt, pepper, and ground fennel. Grill over high heat to desired doneness, about 3 minutes per side for rare. Meanwhile, cook the gnocchi in the boiling water until they float, 2 to 3 minutes. Drain in a collander, and toss in the sauce.

For the salad, toss the mint, green onions, and parsley with the olive oil and a squeeze of lemon juice. Add salt and pepper to taste.

To serve, place a mound of peperonata and some of the goat cheese gnocchi on each plate. Place 2 steaks on top of each serving and garnish with a little mint salad. *Serves 4 as a main course*

Wine-pairing suggestion: 2000 Unti Sangiovese, Segromigno

Left: Straddling the Sonoma-Marin county border is McEvoy Ranch. Originally a dairy farm, today its hills are covered with some eighteen thousand olive trees. Started in the 1980s, McEvoy Ranch produces certified organic extra virgin olive oil. Their on-site olive mills allow the fruit to be pressed immediately after picking, essential for high-quality oil. McEvoy Ranch grows a mixture of Italian olive varieties, including Frantoio, Leccino, Pendolino, Maurino, Coratina, and Leccio del Corno.

Above: Right at the edge of the road that runs through Cotati Valley looms a huge old barn, built in 1868 by the Crane family. The barn now houses outrageously delicious Crane melons, a cross between a Japanese melon and a cantaloupe hybridized by Oliver Crane in the 1920s. Fifth-generation owner Rick Crane explains that during melon season, from September until frost, cars fill the parking lot as buyers prod and sniff the melons, seeking perfect ripeness. Rarely found outside Sonoma County, Crane melons are prized for their flavor and juicy flesh.

Left and top: The grape "crush" is the busiest time in a vineyard. The winemaker decides when to harvest by testing grapes, looking for the perfect balance of acidity and sugar for the grape variety. Once the grapes reach that level of perfection, they must be harvested and crushed quickly to avoid missing their prime.

Workers fill a gondola with Chardonnay grapes that will be used to make sparkling wine. Low-sugar Chardonnay grapes are usually among the first grape varieties harvested. Crews work all day and in shifts through the night under bright lights. A sudden rain, a cold snap, or a broken machine can delay a harvest and impact a vintage.

Above: In contrast to hectic harvesttime, spring in the vineyard is calmer, although there is much work to be done after winter rains, checking the trellis systems before pruning and fertilizing the vines to ensure spring and summer growth.

Preceding pages: The José Ferrer family, producers of Freixenet sparkling wines in Catalonia, Spain, built the Gloria Ferrer Champagne Caves in the southernmost area of the Carneros appellation in 1986. Dug into the hillside are aging cellars where the sparkling wines are fermented to create their famous bubbles. The cool summer breezes blowing in off San Pablo Bay make the Carneros a prime location to grow low-sugar Chardonnay and Pinot Noir grapes used for sparkling wine.

Left: Viansa Winery & Italian Marketplace crowns a hill overlooking the northern-most tip of San Francisco Bay, now a silted-in delta wetlands and bird sanctuary. The winery, reminiscent of a Tuscan villa, is owners Sam and Vicki Sebastiani's homage to their Italian heritage. As third-generation vintners, they have planted Italian grape varieties such as Arneis, Freisa, Nebbiolo, and Sangiovese, as well as Chardonnay and Merlot.

Top: The building at Schug Carneros Estate Winery boasts half-timbered construction, a tip-off to the German heritage of its owner. As at Gloria Ferrer, a hillside location allows the construction of aging caves for the Chardonnay and Pinot Noir wines.

Above: Cline Cellars specializes in Rhône varieties, wine grapes that some experts say match the climate in cooler areas of the county better than more well-known French types such as Cabernet. Cline grows Syrah, Carignane, Mourvèdre, Viognier, and Marsanne.

DELLA FATTORIA

ow wonderful life is, that a young musician and a pre-med student-turned-actress should fall in love and end up in the musician's ancestral home in Petaluma, producing hundreds of crusty, rich-flavored wood-fired loaves six days a week. In a miracle made of dreams and hard work, Ed and Kathleen Weber have turned Ed's family chicken ranch into a compound with houses for their grown children and a bakery built onto the back of their home. Bread from Della Fattoria, or "From the Farm" in Italian, makes Sonoma County residents sigh in ecstasy and look pityingly at out-county residents who are unfamiliar with it.

It's difficult to know whether to start with the breads—the seeded wheat filled with pumpkin seeds, wheat berries, poppy seeds; to the just-slightly crunchy polenta, fabulous for toast; the baguettes, the perfect accompaniment to a fine dinner; or the six other types—or with the bakery, an airy, light-drenched room where their son Aaron and his crew shovel loaves of bread into one of two wood stoves using long-handled baker's peels.

Then there's the story of Kathleen, who took a class with Alice Waters back in the seventies, when she ate goat cheese for the first time, tasted pure fresh olive oil dressing an arugula salad, and decided that she had discovered the world for her. She bought Carol Field's book, *The Italian Baker,* and began to make bread. Her father-in-law described the wood-burning oven in his German village and told her that the best breads came from such a stove. By a fine circumstance, a local builder named Alan Scott was renowned for building wood-burning bake ovens, and soon Kathleen was making bread for her family, then her friends, and then customers who begged for the loaves.

The fine meals Kathleen cooked for her husband and children rubbed off on her son, Aaron, and he started a culinary career. Before long he had introduced his mother to the chef at Sonoma Mission Inn, who ordered bread and advised her as she became a commercial baker. Then Thomas Keller of the award-winning French Laundry restaurant sampled some of her bread

Left and above: Della Fattoria bakery is a family affair, with the ovens built at the back of the Webers' home kitchen. Aaron Weber is the head baker now, taking over for his mother, Kathleen. Aaron's wife, Linda, works in the bakery as well. Their son, Jakob, is in and out all morning long, while Aaron's father, Ed, tends the wood-burning ovens and lends a hand wherever he is needed.

and instantly signed on as a customer. Now, on an average day the bakery turns out 350 loaves of bread for restaurants and a few local food stores. On weekends, eight hundred loaves are baked to be sold at the San Francisco farmers' market as well as to their regular customers. During the week, they sell their loaves at the Sonoma farmers' market, a gala event set up in the grassy plaza in the middle of town. The regular customers line up early, knowing that Della Fattoria always sells out.

What makes this bread so special? Kathleen insists that when making something as simple as bread, the ingredients must be the very best. The Webers make their own starter—no commercial yeast is used—and it is tended two or three times a day, adding more flour as needed. The grains, seeds, and flour are organic, and the flour is milled as freshly as possible. Kathleen stresses that the flavor also comes from the bread mixing method, which is to work the dough very lightly and to let it rest often.

The ovens are fired at night with oak logs for about six hours, and then the ashes are brushed out. The ovens are closed and left empty until baking time—the hour depends upon the amount of loaves to be baked—allowing the ovens to absorb the heat evenly. By mid-morning baking is over, and friends who have been enlisted as drivers drop by to load up their trucks for delivery to markets and restaurants.

And for the future? Kathleen muses about a small restaurant serving wine, bread, cheeses, and olives. Maybe a retail store in the new market planned for the San Francisco farmers' market. For sure, another full-time baker, to give Aaron some additional time off and to increase production.

All this activity bubbles out of the back of the Webers' home, including visits by their grandson, Jakob, who comes in to visit his dad while he's baking, and his mom while she sorts out the orders, grabbing loaves from the tall metal racks to fill great woven baskets or tall brown bags. They still farm the fourteen-acre property, with chickens, sheep, vegetable gardens, grapes, and flowers everywhere. Kathleen is pleased that the ranch still produces food, as it has done from the beginning, feeling that she is carrying on a family tradition. But to a drop-in visitor, it seems like a tiny village in full operation, carrying on a baking heritage as old as humankind.

Above and right: Long baker's peels are used to slide the breads into the blasting hot wood-warmed ovens. The breads cool on tall wire racks after baking, then are bundled into large baskets for restaurant clients or into paper sacks for distribution to stores.

CAMPAGNE BREAD

Della Fattoria

Campagne is a crusty, chewy country French bread. It is delicious and a perfect bread for eating every day.
In our bakery, we use a natural starter. If you already have a starter, then by all means use it in this recipe. If you don't,
then use the biga, an Italian starter that will provide the depth of flavor and rich texture that is so desirable.
—Kathleen Weber, co-owner

Biga

¼ teaspoon active dry yeast
¼ cup warm (105° to 115°F) water
1 cup water (room temperature)
2 cups organic unbleached all-purpose flour mixed with ½ cup organic whole-wheat flour

Dough

¼ cup warm (105° to 115°F) water
1 teaspoon active dry yeast
3¼ cups water (room temperature)
1 scant cup biga, left
4½ cups organic unbleached all-purpose flour
3 cups organic unbleached bread flour
1 tablespoon sel gris (gray sea salt)

🐦 For the biga, sprinkle the yeast over the ¼ cup warm water in a bowl. Stir to dissolve, then stir in the 1 cup water. Stir in the mixed flours ½ cup at a time, then knead the dough in the bowl for about 2 minutes until it is firm but sticky. Oil a large bowl, add the biga, and cover with plastic wrap. Let sit at room temperature for at least 12 or up to 18 hours.

🐦 For the dough, pour the ¼ cup warm water into the large bowl of an electric mixer and sprinkle the yeast over it. Stir to dissolve. Let stand for about 10 minutes, or until foamy. Using the paddle attachment, add the 3¼ cups water and the biga. Then add the all-purpose flour, bread flour, and sel gris. Switch to the dough hook and knead for 2 minutes. Let the dough rest for 10 minutes. Knead again for 2 minutes. Let the dough rest again for 10 minutes and knead again for 2 minutes.

🐦 Wet your hands and, pulling the dough away from the sides of the bowl, turn it out into a well-oiled large bowl and cover with plastic wrap. Let the dough rest for 10 minutes. Wet your hands again and fold the dough by sliding your hand down the inside of the bowl to the center, then lifting and folding the dough. Repeat this process, going around the bowl until the dough has been folded into a bundle. Let the dough rest for 10 minutes. Repeat the folding process 2 times, letting the dough rest for 10 minutes in between. You will feel the dough becoming tighter and more elastic with each folding. Let the dough rest for 1 hour after the final folding, then fold it again. Let the dough rest, covered, for 1½ hours. The dough will be shiny on top and have bubbles underneath the surface.

🐦 To shape the dough, turn it out on a lightly floured surface. Form the dough into a ball, then pat it into a rough square about 2 inches thick. Cover with a cloth and let rest for 10 minutes. Prepare 2 or 3 baskets by dusting them generously with flour. You can use any wicker, straw, or rattan basket with a design. We use the 8-inch-round straw baskets found in Mexican restaurants used to serve tortilla chips. Divide the dough into pieces and shape each into a ball. Dust them lightly with flour, cover with a cloth, and let rest for 10 minutes.

🐦 Place the floured side of a ball of dough down on the work surface, gather all the ends of the dough together, and pinch them closed. Place the ball of dough, seam side down, on the work surface. With cupped hands, start to tighten the dough by pushing the dough away from you while turning it in a circular motion, using the friction of the work surface to seal the pinched bottom. When the top of the ball of dough is stretched taut, place the dough in a prepared basket so it is about half full. Repeat with the remaining dough. Cover all the baskets with a cloth and let the dough rise for 1½ hours. The dough will still be a little shiny, wet, and have a jelly-like consistency. It will mostly retain its shape.

🐦 To bake the bread, place a baking stone, if you have one, on the bottom rack of the oven and remove all the other racks. Preheat the oven to 550°F for 30 minutes. If you don't have a stone, use an up-turned cast-iron skillet for each loaf you are cooking.

🐦 Generously dust a baker's peel or a baking sheet with flour. Line a baking sheet with a thick towel.

Run it under the faucet until the towel is saturated, leaving some unabsorbed water floating on top. Place the pan with the towel on the bottom rack of the oven and quickly close the oven door. This will provide the steam essential for the dough to expand to its potential and develop the proper crust. Moving quickly, invert one of the baskets onto the floured peel by whacking the edge of the basket against the peel to release the dough. It may look a little deflated, but that is normal. Grab a little flour and, holding your arm up high above your shoulder, dust the loaf with it. Using a razor blade, immediately slash the loaf deeply and at a slight angle into a diamond or tic-tac-toe pattern.

⋙ Open the oven door and slide the loaf onto the stone by pulling the peel back with a snapping motion. Slam the door shut to keep the steam inside. Repeat with the remaining loaves.

⋙ Decrease the oven temperature to 450°F and bake for 10 minutes. Remove the baking sheet and towel. Bake for 30 minutes longer, or until the crusts are brown and crackly and the loaves sound hollow when you thump them on the bottom. They should smell like pure heaven. *Makes 2 or 3 round loaves*

CIABATTA

Artisan Bakers, Sonoma

This is the recipe I helped develop with Team USA in 1996 when we won the Bread Bakers Guild gold medal in Paris at the Coupe du Monde. Make the poolish for this recipe at least 12 hours before making the bread.
—*Craig Ponsford, baker-owner*

Poolish
Pinch of active dry yeast
1¼ cups water at room temperature (about 70°F)
2¼ cups bread flour

Dough
¾ teaspoon active dry yeast
1⅓ cups water at room temperature (about 70°F)
4½ cups bread flour
2 tablespoons olive oil
4 teaspoons salt
Poolish, left

⋙ For the poolish, dissolve the yeast in the water in a bowl. Stir in the bread flour until combined. Cover with plastic wrap and let sit at room temperature for at least 12 hours or up to 24 hours.

⋙ For the dough, dissolve the yeast in 1 cup of the water, in the bowl of a heavy-duty electric mixer. Add the flour, olive oil, salt, and poolish. Using the dough hook, mix on low speed for 3 minutes, or until a soft dough is formed.

⋙ Turn the mixer to medium speed and mix for 4 minutes. Turn the mixer to low speed again and add the remaining ⅓ cup water. Mix until the water is incorporated. The dough should be very soft and wet. Place the dough in a lightly oiled bowl and cover tightly with plastic wrap. Let rest at room temperature for 45 minutes.

⋙ Turn the dough out onto a well-floured surface.

Stretch the dough in all directions as far as possible without tearing it, then fold it back on itself. Put the dough back in the bowl, cover, and let rest for 45 minutes. Repeat the stretching and folding 2 more times, allowing 45 minutes of resting time after each fold. After the third cycle, turn the dough out into a heavily floured surface and gently stretch it into a ¾-inch-thick rectangle. Using a sharp knife or a dough scraper, cut the dough into 3 equal rectangles. Place the dough, evenly spaced, onto a parchment-lined baking sheet and cover it with plastic wrap. Let the dough rise at room temperature for 1 hour, or until doubled in size.

⋙ Preheat the oven to 450°F. Bake the dough for 20 minutes, then reduce heat to 425°F and bake for 20 minutes more, or until browned. Remove from the oven and let cool on wire racks. *Makes 3 loaves*

HOG ISLAND OYSTER COMPANY

At first glance, Hog Island Oyster Company looks like a stage set for a movie filmed a hundred years ago. The Hog Shack, a weathered, washed-out white building with faded green trim, where you order and pay for your briny treasures, seems to be sinking into Tomales Bay. Dinghies bob in the cold gray water of the bay, as if they had been there forever. Yet, a mechanical humming and whirring soothed by the sound of running water brings you back to the present as you walk past the entry fence. Water bubbles and foams through large concrete tanks filled with metal net bags, and men dressed in long, thigh-high rubber waders stand near the tanks sorting, cleaning, and counting out oysters or clams to fill netted bags. For an oyster lover, this is heaven.

Hog Island Oyster Company grew from the dream of Michael Watchorn and John Finger, college roommates at University of California, Santa Cruz, who began their careers working at an oyster company in Monterey Bay, just south of the college. Starting their own company up the coast in Tomales Bay was not easy, for oyster farming requires leases from the California Fish and Game Department, and enough bureaucratic whirlpools to sink a new entrepreneur. The two men studied Tomales Bay, a long inlet that cuts open the coastline and runs southeast from the mouth and roughly fifteen miles long to create the Point Reyes Peninsula. They made the canny decision to locate near a big rock called Hog Island, sitting one-quarter mile from the bay's entry into the Pacific Ocean. They reckoned the site would provide fresh, cold salty ocean currents and all the washed-in rich nutrients their oysters could eat. This was a yet unleased area, a "virgin tract," but their petition to open it to oyster cultivation was accepted, and in 1982, the company started harvesting.

The prime location of these beds produces oysters of such sweet brininess that many professionals think Hog Island oysters are among the best in the nation. Carefully chosen to match the ecology of Tomales Bay, they include small and medium Sweetwaters, Kumamotos, larger Atlantics, European Flats, and Manila clams. The range of varieties allows Hog Island to harvest oysters year-round, a concept befuddling to East Coast oyster eaters, trained to resist oysters during the summer months. Yet, the Pacific Ocean, with its frigid summertime temperatures, when matched with the right oyster, provides tasty, firm oysters during the months when Eastern oysters spawn.

Now Michael, John, and Terry Sawyer, who joined the company in 1986, continue to tinker with the details of oyster farming. Michael admits freely that the last twenty years have been a constant trial-and-error process to find the balance between "the biology of the animal with the economy of scale" of their business. They have discovered that to grow flat, handsome oysters they can't cram the growing baskets. The company is building additional water storage tanks so they can harvest during the winter months and keep oysters healthy during the rainy season, when they must now shut down to avoid viral outbreaks from agricultural runoff.

Even though his oysters are sold in restaurants like Gramercy Tavern and the Four Seasons in New York, as well as up and down the West Coast, Michael hopes to open more direct retail outlets. Hog Island sells both fresh and barbecued oysters at the San Francisco farmers' market. The Hog Island Catering Company sets up oyster bars for private parties and special events throughout the Bay Area all year long. The oyster company itself is open to the public from Wednesday to Sunday, drawing a steady stream of visitors who shuck and slurp fresh oysters at the handmade picnic tables, or barbecue them in grills sprinkled around the site. Watching the flow of visitors stepping up to the window at the Hog Shack, it's clear that these oysters are habit forming, but then too, as the sign says on the Hog Island truck filled with freshly harvested wire baskets, "Shellfish are Habitat Forming."

Preceding pages: The tides of the Pacific Ocean bring in cold currents to wash over the oyster beds in Tomales Bay. In Marin County, just south of the Sonoma County line, Hog Island Oyster Company produces oysters in beds next to Hog Island, sited close to the bay's opening into the Pacific Ocean.
Left: Hog Island Oyster Company produces briny-sweet oysters in the ocean-fed waters of Tomales Bay.
Above: Michael Watchorn, one of the three owners, and his son, Gianni, watch over the oyster beds, which are harvested year-round because of the varieties they grow and the ever-cold temperature of the water.

Top: Hog Island raises five different varieties of shellfish, *clockwise, from top center:* European Flat oysters, Kumamoto oysters, Manila clams, Sweetwater oysters, and Atlantic oysters.

Left and above: Cold and wet conditions often make the work of rinsing oyster baskets and sorting oysters for size difficult, although the location of the company on the shores of Tomales Bay is surely one of the most scenic on the coast. Locals and visitors make the Hog Island Oyster Company a destination, using their grills and picnic benches to shuck, cook, and eat on the spot.

Hog Island Oyster Company's Two Most Popular Raw Bar Sauces

Hog Island Oyster Company, Marshall

Each recipe makes enough sauce for 3 dozen shucked oysters. —*Michael Watchorn, owner*

Hog Wash

¼ cup seasoned rice vinegar
¼ cup natural rice vinegar
1 large shallot, peeled and finely diced
1 large jalapeño chile, seeded and finely diced
Leaves from ½ bunch cilantro, minced
Juice of 1 lime

In a small bowl, combine all the ingredients and stir to blend. Refrigerate for 1 hour before serving. *Makes about ¾ cup*

Balsamic Mignonette

½ cup high-quality balsamic vinegar
1 large shallot, peeled and finely diced
Splash of sherry
Freshly cracked pepper

In a small bowl, combine the vinegar, shallot, and sherry. Add pepper to taste and stir to blend. Chill for 1 hour before serving. *Makes about ½ cup*

Barbecued Hog Island Oysters with Roasted Tomato Salsa and Sonoma Dry Aged Jack

Mixx Restaurant, Santa Rosa

We've been serving fresh oysters for ten years. This twist on the traditional recipe was created by the guys who work in the kitchen. It combines the ethnic heritage of the county with local ingredients. —*Dan Berman, chef-owner*

Roasted Tomato Salsa
5 large tomatoes
½ red bell pepper
1 large jalapeño chile
½ large red onion, sliced
2 garlic cloves
Juice of ½ lime
Juice of ½ lemon
Leaves from ½ bunch cilantro, chopped
Salt and freshly ground pepper

24 Hog Island oysters, scrubbed and patted dry
1½ cups (6 ounces) grated Sonoma dry jack cheese
1 cup finely shredded red cabbage
1 cup finely shredded green cabbage
2 lemons, cut into 16 wedges
2 limes, cut into 16 wedges
Cilantro sprigs for garnish

Prepare a fire in a charcoal grill or preheat a gas grill to medium.

For the salsa, grill the tomatoes, bell pepper, jalapeño, onion slices, and garlic for 3 to 5 minutes, or until lightly charred. In a food processor, combine the grilled vegetables and pulse to just past the chunky stage. Do not purée. Add the juices, cilantro, and salt and pepper to taste.

Place the oysters on the grill and cook until just starting to open. Remove from the grill.

Preheat the broiler. Shuck the oysters, leaving them on the bottom shells. Place the oysters on a broiler pan. Top each with a spoonful of salsa and enough dry jack to cover the oyster and salsa (about 1 tablespoon). Place under the hot broiler and cook for 1 to 2 minutes, or until the cheese is golden brown. Remove from the oven.

To serve, sprinkle the red and green cabbage on a large platter. Arrange the oysters on the cabbage. Arrange the lemon and lime wedges in the center and garnish with cilantro. Serve immediately, with the remaining salsa on the side. *Serves 4 as a first course*

Wine-pairing suggestion: Rochioli Sauvignon Blanc, Russian River Valley

Right: A waterside picnic of fresh and barbecued Hog Island oysters.

SONOMA VALLEY

SONOMA VALLEY

The history books credit the Suisun Indians for the word *Sonoma*, which has been translated as "Valley of Many Moons." The Sonoma Valley is twenty-two miles long and just seven miles wide. Winemaking in California started here, home of the state's first two wineries, although many tourists and residents mistakenly credit the Napa Valley as the first location of the state's wineries. At the bottom of the valley lies the Buena Vista Winery and Vineyard, which was licensed in 1857 by a Hungarian, Agoston Haraszthy, who is called the father of California wineries. Reputedly, after drinking some of General Vallejo's wines pressed from Mission grapes, he sailed to Europe in 1861, touring France, Germany, and Italy to collect over 100,000 cuttings of an estimated three hundred different grape varieties and brought them back to California. He selected Sonoma for

its ideal climate, and in 1862 began planting his vineyards with the European varieties, the first in the state. Close by, the Gundlach-Bundschu Winery, the second oldest licensed winery, was founded in 1858 by the Bavarian Jacob Gundlach, who had brought German vine varieties to plant in his new homeland.

The town of Sonoma remains true to its Spanish heritage, having been designed by General Vallejo himself in 1835 with a classically proportioned town square across from the barracks of the former presidio. Around the square, many of the buildings now house winery and cheese stores representing local producers, including Vella Cheese, one of the older artisanal cheese companies in Sonoma County. Their Bear Flag Cheese celebrates the motley crew of Americans who imprisoned General Vallejo in 1846 and declared the Republic of California, which later became a possession of the United States and then the State of California in 1850.

Farther up the valley along State Highway 12, originally a stagecoach road, the climate becomes hotter, wedged on the west by Sonoma Mountain, a sub-appellation, and on the east by the Mayacamas Mountains. The warmth of the valley coaxes out the best in red and heat-loving white grapes, and winery after winery fronting the highway produces Zinfandel, Cabernet Sauvignon, Merlot, and Sauvignon Blanc. To the northwest, in Bennett Valley, lies the Matanzas Creek Winery, with extensive lavender fields planted along with its grapes. The winery yearly celebrates a lavender harvest of some two million flower stems. This herb has moved out of the closet to become the darling of Bay Area chefs, who use it in dishes from grilled chicken to crème brûlée.

In this valley are hundreds of olive trees, part of the agricultural heritage of the Spanish mission fathers and the early Italian immigrants. The Olive Press, a local business selling olive oil and assorted products, not only processes olives from individual producers, but also sponsors community press days, when anyone can bring in freshly picked olives and share proportionally in the resulting shimmering dark green freshly pressed oil. In December, there is a blessing of the olives, a religious ceremony to celebrate the harvest of olives from the original Sonoma Mission's olive trees.

Preceding pages: The Spanish brought mustard plants with them as they migrated up the California coast. Now a typical sight in the early spring, wild mustard grows rampantly between the grapevines and along the country roads.
Left: The barrel room at Kenwood houses wines being aged in oak barrels. The wines mellow and develop their flavor profiles, sometimes for years, depending on the wine. French oak barrels are shipped to Sonoma wineries in large quantities, but local cooperages have sprung up, and a number of vintners now use American oak barrels.
Above: An ornately carved wine cask at Buena Vista, California's oldest premium winery, bears the name of the winery's founder, Count Agoston Haraszthy.

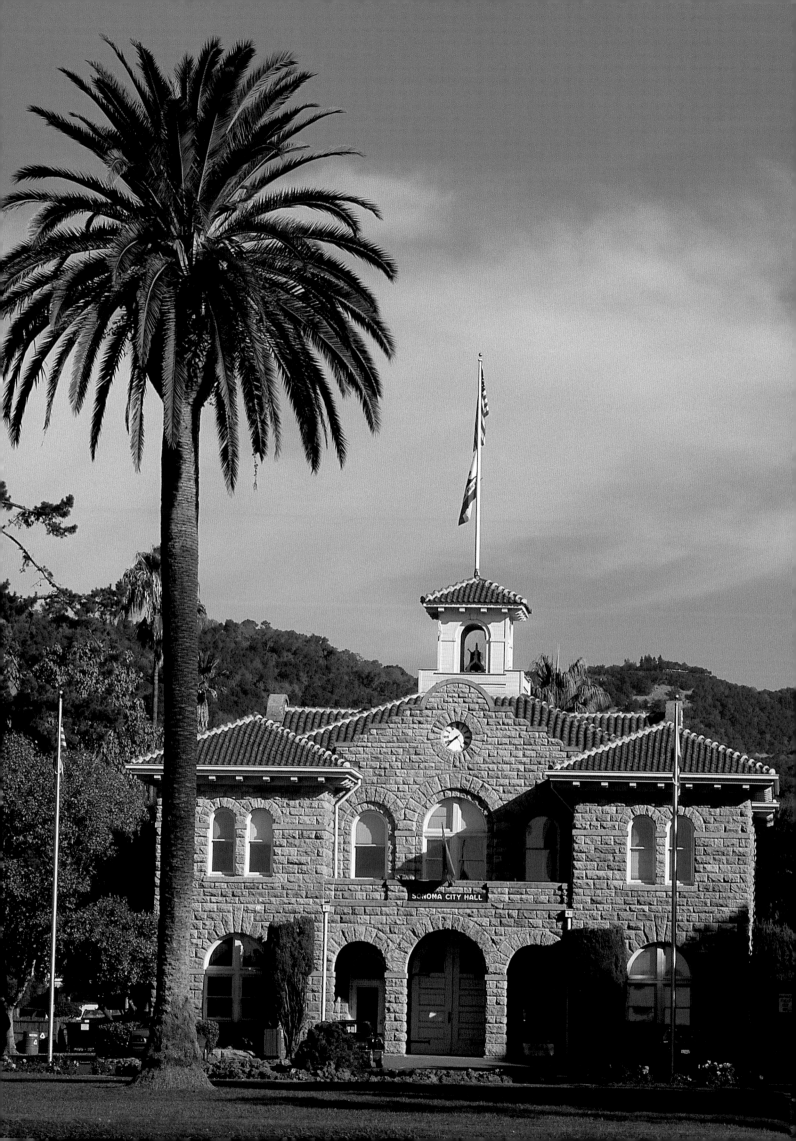

Left: Sonoma City Hall, built in 1906 by San Francisco architect A. C. Lutgens, uses local basalt stone in its Mission-Revival style.

Top and above: General Vallejo originally designed Sonoma Plaza, and the eight-acre site has become the heart of the town, hosting farmers' markets, concerts, and casual picnics. On the square, visitors and locals can patronize the historic Swiss Hotel, built in 1850, and the Sonoma Hotel, built in 1880. Both have popular restaurants specializing in fresh local ingredients.

Above: Located just outside the town of Sonoma, the Sonoma Mission Inn and Spa is a premier wine country retreat. The facilities offer many amenities to soothe the body, and the inn is perfectly situated as a jumping-off spot for exploring Sonoma Valley. The spa is on the site of hot springs first visited by Native Americans and then early Europeans. Artesian mineral water is piped into the bathing pools from eleven hundred feet underground. The inn also features two elegant restaurants specializing in regional California cuisine, each with an extensive Sonoma County wine list.

Right: The climate of the town of Sonoma makes for perfect outdoor dining, as on this patio at Ristorante Piatti, from spring to late fall.

Opposite: The town of Sonoma reflects its Spanish heritage in small alleyways off the plaza.

Opposite and above: Sonoma Plaza stores stock delicious foods for hungry wine-country explorers. The Sonoma Cheese Factory provides outstanding cheeses that pair well with Sonoma wines.

Left: Ignazio Vella, whose father founded Vella Cheese in 1931, is revered for his encyclopedic knowledge of cheese, as well as his historical perspective on artisanal cheese making in Sonoma County. County residents choose Ig's aged dry jack cheese over imported Parmesan for sprinkling on their pasta.

Top, above, and right: Sonoma Valley, snugly placed beyond the direct influence of cold summer-fog breezes, has a warm climate that promotes the luxurious growth of summer vegetables like these, organically raised at Oak Hill Farm just off Highway 12. The same benign conditions nurture the olive trees planted at B. R. Cohn Winery, just a bit south. Their Picholine olives, harvested from trees imported from France 130 years ago, are pressed at the Olive Press in nearby Glen Ellen. The result is French-style B. R. Cohn Sonoma Estate extra virgin olive oil.

Penne Contadina

Della Santina, Sonoma

This is a traditional Italian dish using the great pork sausages from Willowside Meats in Santa Rosa.
—Quirico Della Santina, chef-owner

4 sweet Italian sausages without fennel seed,
   removed from casing
¼ cup olive oil
2 cloves garlic, chopped
4 large fresh sage leaves, chopped
24 ounces canned tomatoes, preferably Italian,
   drained and chopped
1 pound penne pasta
½ cup heavy whipping cream
¼ cup grated Parmesan or
   dry jack cheese

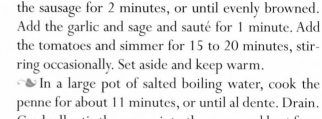

Cut the sausages into 1-inch pieces. In a deep saucepan over medium heat, heat the olive oil and sauté the sausage for 2 minutes, or until evenly browned. Add the garlic and sage and sauté for 1 minute. Add the tomatoes and simmer for 15 to 20 minutes, stirring occasionally. Set aside and keep warm.

In a large pot of salted boiling water, cook the penne for about 11 minutes, or until al dente. Drain. Gradually stir the cream into the sauce and heat for a minute or two. Add the pasta to the saucepan and stir for about 1 minute. Stir in the cheese. Serve at once in warmed shallow bowls. *Serves 4 as a main course*

Wine-pairing suggestion: Gundlach-Bundschu Pinot Noir

Grilled Polenta with Mushroom and Red Wine Ragout

Swiss Hotel, Sonoma

This recipe features two of our favorite local ingredients—Vella cheese and fresh mushrooms
from Gourmet Mushrooms in Sebastopol. —Mary Ellen Oertel, executive chef

Polenta
4 cups water
1 cup heavy whipping cream
¼ teaspoon ground nutmeg
1 cup polenta
1 tablespoon ricotta cheese
2 tablespoons finely grated Parmesan cheese
2 tablespoons grated Vella dry jack cheese
Salt and freshly ground pepper

Olive oil for brushing

Mushroom and Red Wine Ragout
2 tablespoons olive oil
8 ounces whole mushrooms such as cremini, oyster,
   or brown clamshell (see note)
2 ounces shiitake mushrooms, stemmed and sliced
3 tablespoons minced shallots
Salt and freshly ground pepper
½ cup dry red wine
2 cups veal demi-glace
2 tablespoons unsalted butter

Garnish
Shavings of Vella dry jack cheese
Chopped fresh flat-leaf parsley

For the polenta, combine the water, cream, and nutmeg in a large, heavy saucepan. Bring to a boil over medium high heat, taking care not to let it boil over. Gradually whisk in the polenta. Reduce heat to a simmer and cook, stirring frequently, for about 15 minutes, or until the polenta starts to fall away from the sides of the pot. Remove from heat. Stir in the cheeses and salt and pepper to taste. Pour into a 9½ by 12-inch pan. Spread evenly and let cool.

Cut the polenta into triangles and brush with oil. Heat a grill pan over high heat. Grill the polenta for 2 to 3 minutes on one side, or until grill marked.

Meanwhile, for the ragout, heat the oil in a medium sauté pan or skillet over medium heat and sauté the mushrooms and shallots for 2 to 3 minutes, or until tender. Add salt and pepper to taste. Add the wine and demi-glace and cook to reduce slightly. Stir in the butter. Divide the polenta among 4 warmed plates. Pour the ragout over the polenta. Garnish with dry jack and parsley. *Serves 4 as a first course or side dish*

Wine-pairing suggestion: Ravenswood Zinfandel

Note: Brown clamshell mushrooms are available from Gourmet Mushrooms (see Resources, page 223).

Right: Grilled Polenta with Mushroom and Red Wine Ragout

Balsamic Prawns with Chilled Asparagus and Pickled Onion Salad

Ristorante Piatti, Sonoma

*This dish was inspired by the Barbequed Prawns at the legendary Mr. B's on Royal Street
in the French Quarter in New Orleans, where I learned the dish as a young apprentice many years ago.
Its simplistic execution is rivaled only by the powerhouse of flavors it packs.*
—Eric Magnani, executive chef

1 cup thinly sliced red onion
¼ cup rice wine vinegar
12 asparagus spears, trimmed to 5 inches

Prawns
½ cup balsamic vinegar
½ cup dry white wine
¼ cup Worcestershire sauce
1 teaspoon minced garlic
¼ teaspoon red pepper flakes

½ teaspoon minced fresh thyme, oregano, parsley, or basil
2 tablespoons canola oil
20 prawns (jumbo shrimp), shelled and deveined
¾ cup (1½ sticks) unsalted butter, cut into small pieces
Kosher salt

Leaves from 2 heads frisée, torn
Leaves from ½ head radicchio, cut into fine shreds

In a large bowl, combine the onion and vinegar. Let stand for 30 minutes. Blanch the asparagus in salted boiling water for 1 minute, then plunge into ice water for 1 to 2 minutes, or until cool. Pat dry.

For the prawns, combine the vinegar, wine, Worcestershire, garlic, red pepper flakes, and herbs in a small bowl. Heat a large sauté pan or skillet over high heat for 2 minutes, remove from heat and add the oil and prawns at the same time. Return to high heat and sear the prawns on each side for 20 seconds, then add the vinegar mixture. Cook to reduce the liquid by three-fourths. Remove from heat and stir in the butter to make a velvety sauce. Add salt to taste.

Place 3 asparagus spears in the center of each large plate, forming a triangle. Drain the onion slices. Toss the frisée, radicchio, and onion slices together and divide over the asparagus.

To serve, place 5 prawns around each salad. Drizzle a little sauce over the prawns and serve immediately. *Serves 4 as a first course*

Wine-pairing suggestion: 1999 MacRostie Chardonnay

Diver Sea Scallops with Grilled White and Green Asparagus and Oven-Dried Apricots

Santé Restaurant, Sonoma Mission Inn & Spa, Boyes Hot Springs

*I like to use ingredients in their peak season, when the flavors are best. This dish is light and full flavored.
The asparagus spears are crunchy, the scallops are sweet, and the apricot vinaigrette is slightly tart.*
—Michael McDonald, executive chef

Apricot Vinaigrette
1 cup sun-dried apricots
1 cup water
½ cup orange juice
¾ cup Champagne vinegar
1½ cups blended oil
½ cup extra virgin olive oil
1 teaspoon salt

2 fresh apricots, each pitted and cut into 4 wedges
1 tablespoon extra virgin olive oil, plus oil for coating scallops and asparagus
Salt and freshly ground pepper
6 green asparagus stalks, peeled and blanched
6 white asparagus stalks, peeled and blanched
4 large diver sea scallops

For the vinaigrette, combine the dried apricots and water in a saucepan. Bring to a low simmer and cook to reduce the liquid by half. Remove from heat and let cool. In a blender, combine the apricots and their liquid. Add the orange juice and Champagne vinegar. Purée. With the machine running, gradually add the oils to make an emulsified sauce. Stir in the salt and set aside.

Preheat the oven to 300°F. In a small baking dish, toss the fresh apricot wedges with the 1 tablespoon oil and salt and pepper to taste. Bake for about 20 minutes, or until slightly shriveled but still moist. Set aside and keep warm.

In a separate saucepan of salted boiling water, blanch the green and white asparagus for 1 minute, then transfer to an ice-water bath to stop the cooking. Drain and pat dry.

Coat the scallops with oil and season with salt and pepper. In a grill pan over high heat, sauté the scallops until golden, about 1 minute on each side. Transfer to a plate. Coat the asparagus with oil. In the same pan over high heat, grill the asparagus for about 1 minute on each side, or until grill marked.

To serve, divide the asparagus, scallops, and apricot wedges between 2 salad plates. Drizzle ¼ cup of the apricot vinaigrette on each plate. Refrigerate remainder of apricot vinaigrette for up to 1 week. *Serves 2 as a first course*

Wine-pairing suggestion: Matanzas Creek Sauvignon Blanc

Caesar Salad with Tapenade

Sassafras Restaurant, Santa Rosa

This is the number-one-selling item on our menu. People tell us it's the best Caesar salad in town because of the tapenade.
—Scott Snyder, chef

Dressing
1 egg
½ tablespoon Creole mustard
1 to 2 dashes Worcestershire sauce
2 cloves garlic
2 tablespoons red wine vinegar
1 tablespoon fresh lemon juice
½ tablespoon salt
½ tablespoon freshly ground pepper
½ cup olive oil blended with ½ cup canola oil

Tapenade
1½ cups kalamata olives, pitted and finely chopped
2 tablespoons minced garlic
¼ cup capers, chopped
1 tablespoon minced fresh flat-leaf parsley
1 tablespoon minced fresh oregano
1 tablespoon freshly squeezed lemon juice
¼ cup extra virgin olive oil
3 anchovy fillets, mashed to a paste

Leaves from 1 large head romaine lettuce
½ cup shaved Parmesan or dry jack cheese

For the dressing, combine all the ingredients in a food processor. Process until smooth.

For the tapenade, blend the ingredients in a small bowl. Toss the tapenade with the salad greens. Sprinkle with the shaved Parmesan or dry jack cheese. *Serves 4 as a first course*

Wine-pairing suggestion: Murphy Goode Sauvignon Blanc

Grilled Yellowfin Tuna with a Saffron–Citrus Vinaigrette and Charred–Pineapple Salsa

The General's Daughter Restaurant, Sonoma

I love the clean, bright flavors of this dish, and the different combinations work well together. —Joseph Vitale, chef

Saffron-Citrus Vinaigrette

3 cups freshly squeezed orange juice
½ cup thinly sliced shallots
½ cup minced peeled fresh ginger
2 tablespoons sherry vinegar
2 tablespoons dry sherry
½ cup honey
½ cup Chardonnay
1 clove garlic
1 pinch saffron threads
1 cup canola oil
Salt and freshly ground pepper

Charred-Pineapple Salsa

1 red bell pepper
1 jalapeño chile
1 pineapple, peeled, cored, and cut into
   ½-inch-thick rings
½ red onion, finely chopped
Grated zest and juice of 1 lime
½ apple, cored and finely diced
5 fresh basil leaves, minced
Salt and freshly ground pepper

4 ahi (yellowfin) tuna fillets (6 ounces each)
Extra virgin olive oil for coating
Salt and freshly ground pepper

For the vinaigrette, combine all the ingredients except the oil, salt, and pepper in a nonreactive saucepan. Gradually whisk in the oil. Bring to a boil over medium heat and cook to reduce to 1 cup. Season with salt and pepper to taste. Strain through a sieve and set aside.

Prepare a fire in a charcoal grill, preheat a gas grill to high, or heat a grill pan over high heat.

For the salsa, place the pepper, chile, and pineapple on the grill and roast until the pepper and chile are charred all over and the pineapple is browned on both sides. Transfer the pineapple to a cutting board and the pepper and chile to a bowl. Cover the bowl with plastic wrap and let cool to the touch. Meanwhile, cut the pineapple into small dice. Peel and seed the pepper and chile and cut into fine dice.

In a bowl, combine the onion, lime zest and juice, apple, basil, and salt and pepper to taste. Add the diced pineapple, peppers, and chile and mix well. Cover with plastic wrap and set aside. (To prepare ahead, cover and refrigerate for up to 24 hours. Return to room temperature before serving.)

Coat the tuna with olive oil and sprinkle with salt and pepper. Grill for 2 minutes on each side for medium rare. Transfer to warmed plates. Spoon some of the salsa on top of each fillet and drizzle with ¼ cup of the vinaigrette. *Serves 4 as a main course*

Wine-pairing suggestion: Arrowood Chardonnay

SEA SALT–ROASTED SNAPPER

The Girl & the Gaucho, Glen Ellen

This is a great family-style dish. Serve it with roasted potatoes and grilled vegetables. —*John Toulze, executive chef*

Salsa Verde

4 tomatillos, husked, rinsed, and dried

¼ onion

½ poblano chile

4 teaspoons canola oil blended with 2 teaspoons olive oil

3 tablespoons chopped fresh cilantro

¼ teaspoon chipotle powder

1 teaspoon minced garlic

1 tablespoon freshly squeezed lime juice

Salt and freshly ground pepper

4 rosemary sprigs

6 cloves garlic

2 bunches green onions, including green parts

2 whole red snappers (1 to 2 pounds each)

6 cups sea salt

2 tablespoons extra virgin olive oil

For the salsa, prepare a fire in a charcoal grill, preheat a gas grill to medium, preheat the broiler, or heat a grill pan over high heat. Brush the vegetables with oil. Grill until charred, turning as necessary. Let cool. Peel the chile. In a food processor, purée the vegetables. Add the cilantro, chipotle powder, and garlic. Purée again. Stir in the lime juice and salt and pepper to taste.

Put the rosemary sprigs, garlic, and green onions in the cavity of the fish and put the fish in a small square baking pan just large enough to hold them. Cover completely with the salt and bake for 20 minutes, or until opaque throughout. Remove from the oven.

Let the fish rest for 5 minutes. Remove from the salt and brush away any excess salt that has stuck to the outside of the fish. Place the fish on a platter, drizzle with the olive oil, and serve with the salsa verde. *Serves 4 as a main course*

Wine-pairing suggestion: 2000 Matanzas Creek Sauvignon Blanc

POTATOES, GARLIC, AND PROSCIUTTO ON CROSTINI WITH POACHED EGGS AND PESTO CREAM WITH ROASTED GREEN BEANS

Kenwood Inn & Spa, Kenwood

This recipe is a long-standing favorite of our guests. —*Roseann Grimm, owner, and Chris Parry Davies, chef*

Pesto Cream Sauce

1 cup heavy whipping cream

¼ cup pesto

Salt and freshly ground pepper

2 large unpeeled russet potatoes, halved lengthwise

4 tablespoons plus 1 teaspoon olive oil

8 cloves garlic

12 rosemary sprigs

Salt and freshly ground pepper

4 slices crusty French bread

8 ounces green beans

¼ cup distilled white vinegar

4 eggs

4 prosciutto slices

For the pesto cream sauce, put the cream in a medium saucepan and simmer to reduce by half. Add the pesto and simmer for 5 minutes, or until slightly thickened. Add salt and pepper to taste. (To make ahead, let cool, cover, and refrigerate for up to 3 days. Reheat over low heat.)

Preheat the oven to 425°F. Cut each potato half into 4 crosswise pieces. Place in a medium bowl with 3 tablespoons of the olive oil, the garlic, 8 of the rosemary sprigs, and salt and pepper to taste. Toss until completely coated. Spread on a baking sheet and bake for 45 minutes, or until tender.

Brush the remaining 1 tablespoon olive oil on both sides of the French bread. Sprinkle with a little salt and pepper. Place on a baking sheet and toast in the oven for 2 minutes, or until lightly browned.

Cook the green beans in salted boiling water for 4 to 5 minutes, or until crisp-tender. Toss with the 1 teaspoon olive oil and salt and pepper to taste.

To poach the eggs, fill a large sauté pan or skillet half full with water. Bring to a boil and add the vinegar. Lower heat to a simmer. Add the eggs one at a time and poach for 4 minutes. Using a slotted spoon, transfer to a plate.

Place 1 toast a little off center on each plate. Lay a slice of prosciutto across one end of each toast and across the plate. Put a poached egg on one end of each toast and 4 or 5 green beans on the other end. Place 4 slices of potato and 2 garlic cloves next to each toast. Top each egg with 2 tablespoons pesto cream sauce. Garnish with the remaining rosemary sprigs and serve. *Serves 4 as a main course*

Wine-pairing suggestion: Champagne mimosas, made with 1⅓ cups Gloria Ferrer Sonoma Brut sparkling wine mixed with ⅔ cup freshly squeezed orange juice

Berries and Plums with Sangría Reduction

Kenwood Inn & Spa, Kenwood

Our unique wine-country breakfast fruit plate. —Roseann Grimm, owner, and Chris Parry Davies, chef

½ tablespoon dry red wine
1 cup plus 4 tablespoons sugar
3 lemons
1 orange
1½ cups fresh strawberries, hulled and quartered

2 large ripe black plums, halved and pitted
1½ cups fresh raspberries
1½ cups fresh blackberries
4 mint sprigs for garnish

In a large nonstick saucepan, combine the wine and 1 cup of the sugar. Bring to a boil, stirring to dissolve the sugar. Lower heat to a simmer. Using a vegetable peeler, zest the lemons and orange and add the zest to the saucepan. Add the juice from 2 of the lemons and the orange. Simmer to reduce the liquid by half. Let cool, then strain through a sieve, reserving the syrup.

Put the strawberries in a bowl. Squeeze the juice from half of the remaining lemon over them. Add 2 tablespoons of the sugar and stir. Set aside.

Cut each plum half into 4 pieces and put in a medium bowl. Squeeze the juice of the remaining lemon half over them. Stir in the remaining 2 tablespoons sugar. Set aside.

Put the raspberries and blackberries in a medium bowl and add one-third of the sangría reduction. Gently toss to coat the berries. Set aside.

Place one-fourth of the strawberries in the center of each plate. Top with one-fourth of the plums, then one-fourth each of the raspberries and blackberries. Spoon one-fourth of the remaining sangría reduction over each serving of fruit and allow to pool on the plate. Garnish with mint sprigs and serve. *Serves 4 as a dessert*

Honey and Fromage Blanc Ice Cream

Jimtown Store, Jimtown

I first sampled a similar confection at Arzak, a deceptively homey three-star restaurant in the Basque region of Spain, on my surprise-birthday-celebration tour of the region. Of the four dazzling desserts we were served, it was the simplest and the most memorable. Be sure the honey you use is delicious and distinctive. We like Hector's Bees Raw Blackberry Honey from Santa Rosa. —Carrie Brown, owner

1 pound fromage blanc, preferably from Bellwether Farms, at room temperature (see note)
¾ cup honey, such as Hector's Bees Raw Blackberry Honey or a wildflower honey

1 cup heavy whipping cream
1 cup whole milk
1 teaspoon vanilla extract
Pinch of salt

◆ In a food processor, pulse the cheese a few times to whip it. Add the honey and pulse to blend. With the machine running, add the cream, milk, vanilla, and salt through the feed tube. Process until smooth and creamy.

◆ Transfer to the container of an ice cream maker and freeze according to the manufacturer's directions. Serve immediately, or transfer to a storage container, cover, and freeze. Soften the ice cream in the refrigerator for 1 hour before serving. *Makes about 1 quart*

Note: Fromage blanc is a fresh cheese that is like a cross between a ricotta and sour cream. It is tart but not as sour as sour cream. You could substitute a good-quality natural cream cheese (made without gums or stabilizers), but it won't have that subtle, tangy taste.

Goat Cheese Crème Brûlée

John Ash & Company, Santa Rosa

This is a twist on the classic crème brûlée using local ingredients. —Jeffrey Madura, chef

4 cups heavy whipping cream
4-inch piece vanilla bean, halved lengthwise
Pinch of kosher salt
8 egg yolks
1¼ cups sugar

¾ cup crumbled Redwood Hill Farm goat cheese
¼ cup minced fresh lemon thyme
1 teaspoon freshly ground black pepper
Mint sprigs for garnish

◆ Preheat the oven to 300°F. In a large saucepan, combine the cream, vanilla bean, and salt. Cook over medium heat until small bubbles form around the edge of the pan. Remove from heat. Remove the vanilla bean from the hot cream and scrape the tiny seeds back into the cream.

◆ In a large bowl, beat the egg yolks and ¾ cup of the sugar together until pale in color. Gradually stir in the hot cream. Strain through a sieve and skim off any bubbles. Gently stir in the crumbled goat cheese and lemon thyme until the cheese melts.

◆ Divide the mixture among 8 ramekins. Place the ramekins in a roasting pan. Add boiling water to the pan to reach halfway up the sides of the ramekins. Cover the pan loosely with aluminum foil and bake for 55 to 65 minutes, or until the center is just set.

◆ Remove the ramekins from the oven and let cool completely. Cover and refrigerate for at least 5 hours or overnight.

◆ Just before serving, preheat the broiler. Combine the remaining ½ cup sugar and pepper in a small bowl. Sprinkle 1 tablespoon of the sugar mixture evenly over the surface of each custard. Broil 3 to 4 inches from the heat source for 2 to 3 minutes, rotating the ramekins as necessary, until the sugar is caramelized. Take care not to burn. Let sit for 1 to 2 minutes before serving. Garnish with mint sprigs. *Serves 8 as a dessert*

Wine-pairing suggestion: Iron Horse Sparkling Wine or Ferrari-Carano Fumé Blanc

Right: Honey and Fromage Blanc Ice Cream

HECTOR'S BEES

Facing the hives in one of his bee yards, Hector immediately draws the attention of some of the occupants. The hives sit out in an open field in a Santa Rosa neighborhood, and at noon the bees rush in and out of the hive openings. But two or three guard bees come over to Hector, hovering about two feet in front of him. He slowly raises a hand. They buzz for a bit, then fly up slowly, and he correspondingly lifts his hand. The bees leave, reassured that this calm person who smells of honey is no threat to them.

Hector Alvarez is a third-generation beekeeper living in Santa Rosa and caring for more than 500 hives in bee yards throughout Sonoma County. The family tradition began with his grandfather, who raised bees on his farm in Mexico, making hives from hollow tree trunks sealed at the top and bottom with adobe he mixed by hand. Hector's father learned from his father, and when he was working in the Sebastopol apple orchards he collected the wild swarms that he found clumped along the branches of the apple trees, using old apple boxes for hives.

Although Hector is a successful beekeeper today, he had a difficult time getting started in America. After graduating from high school in Mexico, Hector came to Santa Rosa to join his brother, who had stayed after his father returned to Mexico. Hector credits his father for teaching him about the life of the hive, how to raise queen bees, and how to make sure hives thrive and reproduce. But he had no knowledge of the American ways of beekeeping, and his English was very limited.

Left and above: It takes hundreds of bee hours to produce a pint of honey. Their labor is carefully guided by beekeeper Hector Alvarez, who may have to provision a new hive with sugar water in winter, or provide a new queen for the hive. Hector holds up a honey super, the hive's cache of flower nectar, carefully gathered from millions of flowers. The bees fan their wings to dehydrate the nectar in the warmth of the hive until it thickens into honey.

With his brother's help, he secured work at the apple orchard that had employed his father, and to his delight, he found his father's hives, although not in great repair, still active. He worked with them, building new parts from discarded construction wood, and collected honey to share with his friends.

Then Hector discovered the Beekeepers Club of Sonoma County and found mentors in the members, who welcomed him even though his limited English made communication difficult. They steered him to stores where he could purchase the pre-made hive pieces, and they encouraged him to expand his hives and to sell his honey commercially at stores and farmers' markets. A retiring beekeeper taught him how to make candles and turned over his stock of molds along with his tips for making fine candles.

Today, Hector sells honey, comb honey, pollen, propolis—the sticky glue used by the bees to weld their hives together—and pure wax candles at six farmers' markets in Sonoma County. In his small garage, filled to the ceiling and walls, are three different sizes of stainless-steel honey extractors, a stack of hive pieces that runs from floor to ceiling, and thirty or forty hive boxes filled with honey ready to be spun out in the extractors. Along one side is his candle-making bench, with molds, heating pots, and wicks as well as hardening candles.

Now a United States citizen with a wife and two young daughters, Hector has his hands full running his business, checking on his hives, and maintaining the quality of his products. His wife sells at several farmers' markets to give him time to manage the hives, but he works long hours and beekeeping is hard work. He doesn't consider hiring anyone because he worries that they wouldn't do the job to his exacting standards. He says, " I want to keep my customers happy."

Above and right: Hector Alvarez owns bee yards all over Sonoma County. Each one produces honey subtly flavored by the specific flowers in the pastures and fields bordering the yard. A hive contains two or more bottom boxes that house the eggs and brood (the baby bees), the queen, and all the worker bees and drones (the few males responsible for inseminating a virgin queen when she emerges from her special cell). A wire rack, called a queen excluder keeps the queen from laying eggs in the chambers above the rack. Consequently, these chambers hold only honey. This system allows the beekeeper to draw off honey without killing any hatching brood. Hector's bee business is a family affair, and his wife and daughters, *above,* staff the booth at farmers' markets while he travels the county working his beehives.

Preceding pages: Wineries have become travel destinations with glorious gardens as well as delicious wines. Matanzas Creek Winery has extensive plantings of lavender, used for its culinary and aromatic properties and celebrated in a yearly Lavender Festival when the plantings are at the height of bloom.

Top, above, and right: Tractor-pulled trams take visitors around the gardens and vineyards of Benziger Family Winery during wine-tasting tours. The Benzigers bought a Sonoma Valley property, originally a land grant traded to Julius Wegener, a carpenter, in lieu of payment for his services building General Vallejo's original home. Today, the Benziger family produces a range of typical California wines, including Sauvignon Blanc, Merlot, Zinfandel, and Cabernet Sauvignon.

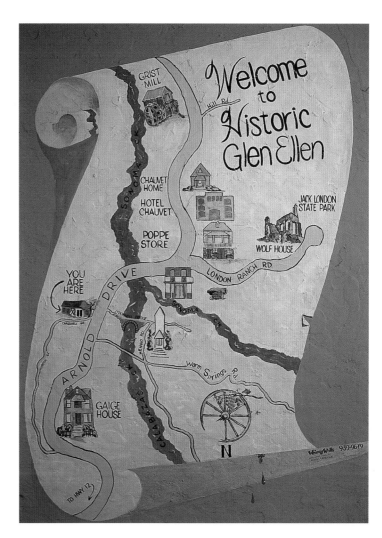

Left, top, and above: The town of Glen Ellen, on Sonoma Creek, grew up around General Vallejo's sawmill. The sleepy village changed when a narrow-gauge railroad began bringing passengers up from San Francisco. By 1879, its reputation was diminished by bawdy bars and dance halls. Jack London came to visit and stayed to establish his Beauty Ranch a short way up the valley in 1909. Now the Jack London Historic State Park, the ranch can be explored by horseback, in much the same way Jack London himself roamed the valley. Currently, the town is edged by wineries and is home to elegant restaurants, chic boutiques, and bed-and-breakfast inns.

SEBASTIANI

VINEYARDS

ESTABLISHED
1904

Left: The stained-glass windows at Sebastiani Vineyards welcome visitors to one of California's oldest vineyards, established in 1904 by Samuele Sebastiani. Sam arrived in the Bay Area from Italy in 1895, and after working at a variety of odd jobs, went back to his Tuscan vocation of wine making, establishing a tradition that is now in its third generation.

Above: A relative newcomer to the Sonoma Valley, Imagery Estate Winery, started by the Benziger family, houses a contemporary tasting room in the midst of a lively art gallery displaying original sculpture and art commissioned for its signature wine labels. Wine racks displaying their single-vineyard wines, unique glassware, and wine accessories are silhouetted in the winery's modern interior.

Above and opposite: The wine master's task is to judge the grapes' development as they mature from flowering to berry, go through their veraison stage, when the grapes change color, and then to the engustment, the last forty-five days when the grapes achieve maximum development of flavor and aroma compounds, and their sugar and acid balances portend a delicious final product. Red wines, like those made from these Zinfandel grapes at Kenwood Winery, are crushed and left temporarily with their skins and seeds to develop flavor and color, while white wines are crushed and the juice strained off.

Right: Of newer vintage is Ravenswood, established in 1976, well known for its fine Zinfandel, a red, fruity, spicy wine unique to California. The raven-inspired winery logo can be seen by visitors in one of the beautiful etched-glass windows of the tasting room.

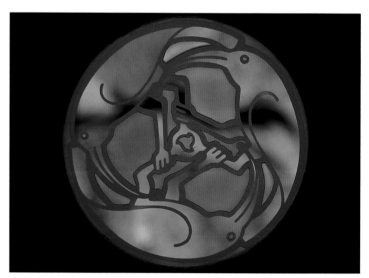

Top: Wineries line both sides of the old stagecoach route, now State Highway 12. Kunde Estate Winery just south of the little town of Kenwood is one of the older ones; the original stone winery dates back to 1882, although now it is just a shell.
Above: The gardens and fountain of Landmark Vineyards frame a breathtaking view of the valley and mountains beyond, and are also home to courts for bocce ball, the Italian game similar to lawn bowling.
Right: Arrowood Vineyards & Winery was founded in 1987 by Richard Arrowood, the former winemaker of Chateau St. Jean, and his wife, Alis Demers Arrowood.

Preceding pages and above: Chateau St. Jean is one of the largest wineries in the valley and a member of the Beringer Wine Estates. Originally, it was a private home on 250 acres of land. The large tasting room was formerly the spacious living room. *Right:* Extravagant rose gardens surround the Gothic-style buildings at Ledson Winery and Vineyards. In France, rosebushes were traditionally planted at the ends of vine rows as a host for beneficial insects and a lure for pests. In the Sonoma Valley, you can often see this tradition continued in the vineyards and enhanced by glorious plantings around winery buildings as well.

Opposite: At the foot of the Mayacamas Mountains lies St. Francis Winery and Vineyards. The spacious new Spanish-style building in the heart of central Sonoma Valley is home to a beautiful tasting room overlooking vineyards and gardens. The room serves up St. Francis Chardonnay, Cabernet, Merlot, and Zinfandel, but for an additional fee, guests may experience the reserve tasting room, with paired samples of wine and food prepared by their executive chef, including some of their reserve wines and even a St. Francis port.

WESTERN SONOMA

From the bustling town and county seat of Santa Rosa, the fertile Santa Rosa plain runs westward to the small towns of Sebastopol and Forestville. There, hemmed in on the north by the Russian River, the land crumples into hills and finally forms the heavily forested, steep ravines of the redwood coast. The little town of Occidental lies in a cleft surrounded by redwood trees replanted and regrown from the stands of virgin forests that were the source of San Francisco's original redwood-timbered buildings, mostly lost in the earthquake of 1906.

The plant hybridizer and propagator Luther Burbank moved to Santa Rosa and set up his experimental gardens in Sebastopol in 1875 because the soil and the climate produced what he described as the perfect growing conditions— "the chosen spot of all this earth." His plant introductions ranged from the spineless cactus (his hope for a low-water crop to feed cattle) to countless hybrids such as the Shasta daisy, the pluot (a cross between the apricot and the plum), and the superb Santa Rosa plum. Burbank also played an important role as a nurseryman, bringing in trees to support the growing apple industry at the end of the nineteenth century.

Indeed, the climate and the soil of western Sonoma County have spawned generations of farmers to hoe, plant, and till this fertile region. The first European farmers, the Russians, planted just inland to escape the cold summer fog. Then, when many Italians settled here after failed careers as gold miners, they planted grapes. Vineyards prospered along the reaches of the Russian River until phylloxera struck in the late 1800s and the dying vines were pulled out to be replaced by hops, prunes, and apples. The dried-fruit business burgeoned before refrigeration, and both prunes and Gravenstein apples became the farmer's standby.

Left: Whether sparkling wines, Viognier, Sauvignon Blanc, or Chardonnay, the award-winning white wines of western Sonoma team deliciously with food, as visitors to the tasting room at J Wine Company will attest. Many wineries present tasting menus for their visitors, to acquaint their palates with the subtleties of matching wines with food. J Wine Company presents small, elegant treats, matched to bring out the best in both food and wine.
Above: Luther Burbank's home and gardens have become a public park close to the center of Santa Rosa. Visitors to the home have the chance to see many of his plant hybrids growing on site. Burbank became an agricultural spokesperson for Sonoma County at the turn of the nineteenth century. His farming tradition is carried on today by many of the small farms and specialty nurseries in the county.

Nowadays, farming in this region includes apples and flowers, as well as ducks and turkeys. As in the southern part of the county, dairy animals thrive here because the cooler air from the coast aids in milk production beneficial to dairies like Redwood Hill Farm, Bodega Goat Cheese, and Bellwether Farms.

Hidden away in the hills above the county's coast are vineyards of the Sonoma Coast appellation. These vineyards receive twice as much winter rain and wind as those inland, and some grapes must endure chilly morning temperatures when the summer fog blots out the sun for much of the morning and often again in the late afternoon. But many of the vineyards are planted above the fog line, where the fog burns off quickly in the morning and the temperatures are higher. The Sonoma Coast appellation is very promising and currently the largest appellation in the county in square miles, though it has the smallest planted acreage, just 7,000 acres.

Bodega Bay, first discovered in 1775 and named after its Spanish discoverer, Don Juan Francisco de la Bodega y Cuadra, is the busiest fishing port on the coast between San Francisco and Eureka, the last big California town to the north. Commercial fishing boats bring their harvest into Bodega Bay, which is protected from winter storms and summer winds by a sandy hook known as Bodega Head. Boats net and catch herring, king salmon, albacore, Pacific halibut, rockfish, and Dungeness crab, all rightly considered world-quality seafood. At wharves and docked boats around the harbor, residents buy freshly caught crabs and fish, while smoked salmon and cooked crabs are sold at small shops along the road.

Locals will tell you that the sand dab, which compares to English sole but is rarely seen outside California, is superb and sought after in fish markets in the county. Equally beloved are the blue-black Pacific mussels that cling tightly to beach rocks, but are open to plunder at low tide in the winter for those willing to bear the chill of the water to pry them off.

The Russian River Valley appellation runs north of Bodega, its borders defined by the fog's reach. The district's lines now include the sub-appellations of Green Valley and Chalk Hill, and at its eastern edge it touches the Dry Creek and Alexander Valley appellations. The coastal climate guarantees a cool growing season, making the area prime territory for Pinot Noir and Chardonnay.

Top, above, and right: Kendall-Jackson's California Coast Wine Center lies off Highway 101 and is replete with elegant gardens and a wine-tasting center promoting their wines as well as those from some smaller boutique wineries that are owned by Kendall-Jackson. The gardens around the winery are exceptional, particularly the culinary garden showcasing herbs and vegetables that pair well with white or red wines. Every summer, the gardens become the site of the Heirloom Tomato Festival, with local artisanal food producers offering tastes of their products, including many varieties of tomatoes never found in supermarkets.

Left and above: The Russian River Valley appellation celebrates yearly with a barrel tasting of wines that have not yet been bottled. Tastings also include bottled vintages from previous years. Wines in barrels are in the aging stage of their evolution, after they have been picked and crushed, and the fermentation with the alcohol-producing yeasts has occurred. While the wine rests in the barrel, its flavors mingle and its chemistry stabilizes. This stage can take place in large or small wooden barrels, such as these containing Pinot Noir at Davis Bynum Winery, or in large stainless steel tanks.

SIMPLE GARDEN TOMATO SOUP

Madrona Manor, Healdsburg

When you have more tomatoes in the garden than you know what to do with, this is the perfect recipe.
—Jesse Mallgren, executive chef

¼ cup extra virgin olive oil
1 yellow onion, thinly sliced
2 cloves garlic
2 pounds heirloom tomatoes, coarsely chopped
¼ cup fresh whole basil leaves
Salt and freshly ground pepper

~ In a large saucepan, heat the oil over low heat. Add the onion and garlic. Cover and cook for about 20 minutes, or until the onion and garlic are soft. Add the tomatoes and cook, uncovered, for 20 minutes, or until soft. Turn off heat, add the basil and cool for 30 minutes.

~ Pass the soup through a fine-meshed food mill or purée in a blender. Strain through a fine-meshed sieve. Add salt and pepper to taste. Heat and serve with your favorite bread. *Serves 4 as a first course*

Wine-pairing suggestion: Iron Horse Sparkling Wine

PUMPKIN SOUP

St. Francis Winery Kitchen, Santa Rosa

Here is a simple and light fall soup to begin your Thanksgiving dinner. This soup has Italian roots because of the riso, pumpkin, and porcini mushrooms and, of course, the Parmesan served alongside. —Todd Muir, chef

½ cup extra virgin olive oil
1 red onion, diced
6 cloves garlic, minced
1 small sugar pumpkin (2 to 3 pounds), peeled, seeded, and diced
1 savoy cabbage, cored, large ribs removed, and chopped
1 ounce dried porcini mushrooms, soaked in hot water for 30 minutes, drained, and chopped
1 pound riso pasta
3 quarts chicken stock, preferably homemade
Salt and freshly ground pepper
Grated imported Parmesan cheese for garnish
Chopped fresh flat-leaf parsley for garnish

~ Heat the olive oil in a heavy 8-quart soup pot over medium-high heat. Add the onion and garlic and sauté for about 3 minutes, or until the onion is translucent. Add the pumpkin, cabbage, mushrooms, and pasta. Cook, stirring constantly, for 10 minutes. Add the chicken stock and bring to a boil. Lower heat to a simmer and cook for about 9 minutes, or until the pasta is al dente. Add salt and pepper to taste. Serve in soup bowls, garnished with Parmesan cheese and parsley. *Serves 6 as a first course*

Wine-pairing suggestion: 2000 St. Francis Sonoma County Chardonnay

GRAVENSTEIN APPLE BABY GALETTES

Downtown Bakery & Creamery, Healdsburg

This is one of the most popular items on our menu. We sell hundreds of galettes a day and make them 365 days a year. Many varieties of fruit can be substituted for the apples (rhubarb, berries, peaches, apricots, nectarines, pears, and so on). The amount of sugar may need to be adjusted slightly depending on the sweetness of the fruit. For very juicy fruit, add an additional teaspoon of flour to the flour spread on the bottom of each tart before the fruit is added.
—Kathleen Stewart, owner-chef

Galette Dough

2 cups all-purpose flour

1 teaspoon sugar

¼ teaspoon salt

¾ cup (1½ sticks) cold unsalted butter, cut into small pieces

½ cup cold water

Filling

1 pound Gravenstein apples, peeled, cored, and cut into ¼-inch-thick slices

4 teaspoons flour

4 teaspoons plus 4 tablespoons sugar, plus more for sprinkling

4 pinches ground cinnamon

2 tablespoons unsalted butter, melted

For the dough, combine the flour, sugar, and salt in a bowl. Stir to blend. Using a pastry cutter or your fingers, cut or rub in the butter until the mixture looks like cornmeal. Gradually stir in the water just until the mixture holds together. On a lightly floured surface, form the dough into a ball, press into a disk, and wrap in plastic wrap. Refrigerate for at least 30 minutes, or up to 1 hour.

Divide the dough into 4 pieces. On a lightly floured surface, form each piece into a ball and roll into a 6-inch-diameter round about ⅛ inch thick. Place on a baking sheet lined with parchment paper and refrigerate while preparing the filling. It is very important to keep this dough chilled at all times.

For the filling, preheat the oven to 400°F. Divide the fruit into 4 portions, about ¾ cup per tart. Remove the galette dough from the refrigerator and sprinkle 1 teaspoon flour and 1 teaspoon sugar in the center of each round, spreading to cover the entire round. Place 1 portion of the apples in the center of each round, leaving a 1-inch border. Sprinkle 1 tablespoon sugar and a pinch of cinnamon over each portion of apples. Fold the pastry border over the apples, pleating as you go. Brush the pastry edge with the melted butter and sprinkle with a little more sugar. Bake for 20 to 25 minutes, or until the apples are tender and the pastry is browned. Transfer to a wire rack. Serve warm or at room temperature. *Makes four 4-inch tarts; serves 4 as a dessert*

Wine-pairing suggestion: Arrowood Vineyard Select Late Harvest Riesling

DEVOTO GARDENS

Devoto Gardens sits atop Gold Ridge just outside the town of Sebastopol in prime Gravenstein apple country. In fact, Gold Ridge was the area where George Griffith began the commercial production of Gravenstein apples in Sonoma County in the mid-nineteenth century. The Gravenstein, an heirloom apple mentioned in seventeenth-century literature, has a sweet flavor when just picked from the tree, and a meltingly superb texture when cooked. As a dried fruit or a juice apple, it excels. Tales vary as to how the apple came to Sonoma County, but probably a tree was brought by an international traveler to the Russian settlement at Ft. Ross, where some of the pear trees from the original orchard still exist. Regardless, the Gravenstein's growing requirements perfectly match Sonoma County climate, particularly around Sebastopol, and they became sought after as a culinary delicacy. The apples brought good income to their growers in the first half of the twentieth century because of

their value as a dried or juice crop, important in pre-refrigeration days. Because they produce for only a short season and are notoriously perishable, they are less well known throughout the United States.

Houses have supplanted some of the original orchards along the Ridge, but Stan Devoto and his wife, Susan, farm twenty ridgetop acres, leasing an additional fifteen acres of apples on a different property. Devoto Gardens produces more than forty different varieties of apples. Planted along the crest of the hill, the trees run across the downslope from north to south. The view looks out to the whole range of eastern mountains that edge the Sonoma plain, even allowing a glimpse of Mount St. Helena in Napa County.

Stan and Susan Devoto were living in El Cerrito, California, in 1976 when friends bought property in Sebastopol. Both dedicated gardeners, they decided they were ready for a lifestyle change, too. They purchased a starter apple orchard with a house, on 2½ acres on Gold Ridge Road. Susan gave up her job as a bank administrator, but Stan continued with carpentry work as they learned to farm their new property. Stan says they asked a lot of questions to learn about apple trees, and Susan took agricultural classes at

the junior college. After a study project on how to make money farming, she suggested they grow cut flowers. Soon they discovered that a property further up on Gold Ridge was for sale, this time with twenty acres of apples, and they moved up the hill to their current location.

They have replanted their apples numerous times, pulling out less-productive old trees and grafting new varieties on tree bases as more interesting apples became available. Stan worked with a well-known local old-timer to graft his stocks of unusual heirloom apples onto his more pedestrian trees. He came across one called Hawaii, which is now a best-seller for him, an intensely sweet apple with tropical flavors of pineapple. In a good year, his Fuji apples stay on the trees until December, so he can take apples to farmers' markets that put long-stored supermarket apples to shame.

Sonoma County has a history of changing its produce to meet market demands. Stan and Susan, watching the rise and fall of apple prices, have diversified by growing cut flowers. With publicity about the exquisite flavors of heirloom apples, the public's interest has been piqued, and his heirloom apple business does well.

In the family partnership, Stan runs the field crews, following set patterns of winter pruning and spraying, early-summer fruit thinning, picking, and light summer pruning. At the same time, the big greenhouses must be maintained for starts of cut flowers; the fields planted with cosmos, sunflowers, and a dozen other types; and the flowers picked for the thirteen farmers' markets a week. Susan runs the business end of the farming operation, handling the orders, billing, and financial records.

As for the future, Stan hopes he and Susan can cut back on the business a bit. Susan loves to travel, and he is a dedicated mountaineer. If he had his choice, he would work only with apples, because the maintenance schedule is easier than the day-to-day work of growing cut flowers. And Stan loves apples. Seeing him walk down the rows of trees, scanning each tree, and with almost an involuntary movement pulling off the little apples that he knows will never swell to full size while at the same time extolling the virtues of each variety, you know that these heirloom apples have one of their best fans in Stan.

Left and above: Stan Devoto is happiest in his apple orchards and on vacation climbing mountains. Sonoma County apple orchards are a familiar sight in the county. Both modern and heirloom apples can be found in all the local farmers' markets.

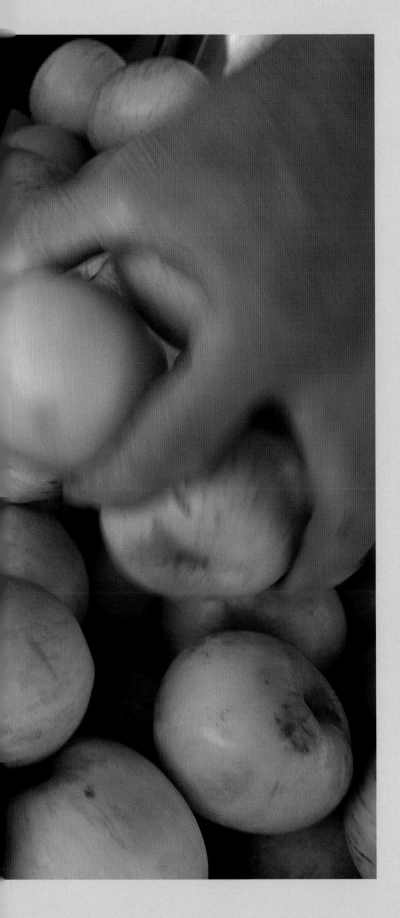

Left, top, and above: Devoto Gardens follows the routine of the seasons, from pruning apple trees in early winter to delivering flowers to farmers' markets throughout the summer. The apple harvest starts in August with early varieties like Gravensteins, *left,* and goes through November with late-season apples, such as Fujis. The Gravenstein Apple Fair, held in August every year, celebrates the beginning of the apple harvest. Gravenstein apples can be eaten fresh, pressed for juice, or cooked for applesauce, pies, and cakes.

KOZLOWSKI FARMS

Home Made

PIES
COOKIES
TARTS
and more....

Apple Bags
4 pounds
$3.00 each
75¢ lb.

Apples
40 pounds
$ 25.00

KOZLOWSKI FARMS
Sonoma County Classics

Carmen and Anthony Kozlowski met and married some fifty years ago, eventually buying a home with an orchard between the town of Sebastopol and the village of Forestville. The property was planted with Gravenstein apples but the trees were old and weak and the Kozlowskis wanted to replant with new, vigorous ones. Tony decided to try an experiment, by planting berry bushes between the rows of spindly new trees. In the end, he had some twenty acres of raspberries, blackberries, and apples. Apples take seven years to come into production, and he reasoned that the berries, quick to produce, would bring in a cash crop until the apples matured. When the berries began to blossom and fruit, Kozlowski Farms came into being.

What to do with all those berries? Tony had chosen vines that produced crops twice a summer! They sold berries to everyone they could, but the flood of fruit continued. Carmen, energetic and resourceful, decided to make jam, and in the cool of the summer mornings, everyone in the family rallied round to stir huge vats in the family kitchen and to bottle up the jam into jars. A roadside sign and a table filled with jars of jam were the start of Kozlowski Farms.

Today, the roadside table has become a tidy store, reached by driving through a narrow alley of the last of the apple trees. Most of the orchard has been replanted with Pinot Noir grapes that are harvested for the David Bruce winery. The grapes grown here are part of the Russian River Valley appellation. Some seventy products are produced in the bright red apple-packing barn, now converted to store, office, production kitchen, cooler, and mailing depot. There are jams and jellies, fruit spreads (jams sweetened by apple juice, not sugar), vinegars, salad dressings, and apple and fruit pies. What they don't grow themselves, the family buys from small farms, with much of the fruit coming from producers in the Northwest that have been with them for years.

As with many businesses, there were difficulties along the way. After the unexpected death of Tony twenty years ago, Carmen called a family council to say that the only way she could continue Kozlowski Farms would be if her three children, Carol, Cindy, and Perry, would take over the business. The pact has lasted, with Carol Kozlowski-Every doing the marketing, Cindy Kozlowski-Hayworth handling the office, and Perry Kozlowski overseeing all production.

Carol predicts that the business will continue, fueled by the siblings' love of the land and their dedication to family. Carmen Kozlowski was the first woman in Sonoma County to be presented by the Harvest Fair with the award of Lifetime Contributor to Agriculture, and the family treasures its agricultural heritage, engaging all the grandchildren in the business—two granddaughters have summer jobs in the store—and involving themselves in community work, volunteering their time on the Harvest Fair Board and many other Sonoma agricultural organizations.

Carol says of her family, "We are hands-on people," meaning that if there is work to be done, they will do it, themselves.

Left: Kozlowski Farms still makes all its products on the site of the family home, where an old barn has been converted to a kitchen. Visitors can purchase freshly made jams, condiments, or fresh berry pies, or just sit outside enjoying a bottle of Gravenstein apple juice.
Above: The Kozlowski family: bottom row, Kimberly Knechtle and on Carol Kozlowski-Every's lap, Kimberly's son, Dyllan Knechtle, Carmen Kozlowski, Cindy Kozlowski-Hayworth; top row, Perry Kozlowski and Janae Kozlowski.

Top, above, and right: Although the business started with jam, Kozlowski Farms is now also known for its spiced vinegars, salad dressings, and fruit spreads: wonderful jams made with apple juice instead of sugar. Fresh fruit pies are available at the farm store.

Above and right: County fairs and festivals celebrate the agricultural roots of Sonoma County throughout the year. Grape-stomping contests, *above,* provide amusement for watchers and stompers alike.

Opposite: The Sonoma County Fair promotes agriculture with a host of exhibits for city visitors and activities for 4-H members and Future Farmers of America. Young people raise rabbits, chickens, pigs, goats, sheep, llamas, alpacas, and cows—dairy or beef—to show during the fair. They often sleep at the fair while their animals are on exhibit, and culminate a year of work presenting their washed, trimmed, and polished animals in the show ring. The animals are auctioned off with spirited bidding by local stores to raise money for the young farmers.

Top: Bruce Campbell started in 4-H raising sheep to show at local fairs. Now the owner of C. K. Lamb, he ships lamb to restaurants nationally, and volunteers his time as an auctioneer during 4-H auctions.

Above: Saralee McClelland Kunde, related by birth and marriage to two prominent local farm families, ran the Sonoma County Fair for years. She is an outstanding promoter of agriculture in the county, through her winery business and her promotion of Russian River Valley–appellation events and 4-H projects and by encouraging culinary events that link farmers and chefs with county visitors.

Right: Working with the animals teaches young farmers the discipline of daily feeding and attentive care for their animals as they grow.

Left and above: A young champion pig farmer, *left,* and Willie Benedetti, owner of Willie Bird Turkeys, *above.* Many of the adults working in Sonoma County agriculture today grew up belonging first to a 4-H group, then to Future Farmers of America. These leaders, whether raising dairy animals, poultry, pigs, chickens, or ducks, grew up showing together at the various fairs, and this network of close friends and acquaintances helps keep the county agricultural community thriving. Benedetti started in 4-H, and then began raising and selling turkeys at age fourteen. Now he sells about 100,000 turkeys a year nationwide.

SONOMA POULTRY COMPANY
Liberty Duck

As far as the eye can see down the shady chicken house, white ducks with bright orange beaks sit contentedly at their leisure, occasionally uttering soft quacks. The long, narrow barn, converted to house ducks, has at least a foot of straw on the ground, and barrels of food provide self-feeding centers. Water pipes with special feeders allow the ducks to slake their thirst with water. When visitors walk through the barn, the ducks rise up and swirl out of the way in loud quacking alarm, settling back on the ground after the visitors pass by.

These are Liberty ducks, the products of Jim Reichardt's Sonoma Poultry, a company that has produced ducks for chefs and restaurant-goers since 1992. Jim's great-grandfather started raising ducks in San Francisco in 1901 and part of his family continues in the business. Jim created his own company to produce a different product from his family's ducks. His Peking ducks from a Danish strain are harvested slightly older and larger than most commercial ducks—at about nine weeks and five or six pounds, which takes more feed and consequently more expense—but Jim prefers the taste of the meat and the generous proportion of meat to bone and fat than in ducks harvested younger and lighter.

Jim raises some twenty-thousand ducks at a time, driving to the Petaluma post office to pick up weekly shipments of ducklings hatched in Salinas, California, two thousand ducklings a shipment. The little balls of golden fluff start off in a heated room warmed to simulate the cozy temperature under a nesting mother duck, and after about a week move into the next room with less heat before they are transferred to an unheated barn. Jim finds that given enough food, water, and room to waddle about, the ducks are healthy and grow quickly, with minor interference from him.

Sonoma Poultry is a remarkable business that thrives with almost no marketing, and no advertising, just word of duck. Selling ducks primarily wholesale and always fresh, never frozen, Jim gets phone calls from chefs all over America. He raises as many ducks as he can, and has as many customers as he can handle. In the future, he would like to set up his own processing plant and work with other Sonoma County purveyors to establish a distribution system. He dreams of trucks that would come to him and whisk his ducks off to his customers, saving him long hours of driving. Still, he loads up his van with ducks and takes off to deliver them to the Bay Area, where he is greeted warmly by chefs who can't wait to serve up Liberty ducks in their restaurants.

Left and above: Tiny, fluffy yellow ducks arrive in cartons at the post office. Jim Reichardt, owner of Sonoma Poultry, picks the ducks up, and starts them on their way.
Overleaf: The ducks live in airy, spacious barns, with soft straw underfoot, and as much food and water as they need.

Duck Confit and Farfalle

Swiss Hotel, Sonoma

Here at the Swiss Hotel, we use several local organic produce companies, one of which is Oak Hill Farm, that provide us with delicious seasonal vegetables.
—Mary Ellen Oertel, executive chef

Duck

4 Liberty brand duck legs, available from Sonoma Poultry Company

2 tablespoons kosher salt

1 teaspoon black peppercorns, crushed

1 tablespoon juniper berries, crushed

4 large rosemary sprigs

2 cups duck fat, available from your butcher or Sonoma Poultry Company

Sauce

¼ cup olive oil

1 leek, white part only, chopped

8 ounces English peas, shelled and blanched

8 ounces mushrooms, sliced

2 cups coarsely chopped baby spinach or Swiss chard

12 asparagus spears, trimmed and cut into 1-inch pieces

2 cups duck or chicken stock

1 cup veal demi-glace

3 Roma tomatoes, peeled, seeded, and finely chopped, or ½ cup good tomato sauce

1 tablespoon minced fresh thyme

1 tablespoon minced fresh oregano

3 tablespoons unsalted butter

Salt and freshly ground pepper

12 ounces dried farfalle (bow-tie) pasta

For the duck, rinse the legs and pat them dry. Place, skin side down, on a wire rack set on a baking sheet. Sprinkle the salt, peppercorns, and juniper over the legs. Place a rosemary sprig on each leg. Cover with parchment paper and another baking sheet. Weight with a heavy object, such as a cast-iron skillet, and refrigerate for about 24 hours.

Preheat the oven to 300°F. Rinse off the legs and pat them dry. In a heavy, 4-inch-deep roasting pan, melt the duck fat. Add the legs, cover with aluminum foil, and braise for 1½ to 2 hours, or until very tender.

Drain off the duck fat and reserve for another use. Let the legs cool to the touch. Pull the meat from the bones and discard the bones, or gently twist the thigh bone out and leave the leg intact, depending on your serving preference.

For the sauce, heat the oil in a large sauté pan or skillet over high heat and sauté the leek, peas, mushrooms, spinach, and asparagus for about 45 seconds. Add the stock, demi-glace, tomatoes, and herbs. Cook to reduce to a sauce consistency. Stir in the butter and salt and pepper to taste. Set aside and keep warm.

In a large pot of salted boiling water, cook the pasta for about 10 minutes, or until al dente. Drain and toss with the shredded duck meat and sauce, or serve the boned duck leg over the sauced pasta. *Serves 4 as a main course*

Wine-pairing suggestion: Cline Cellars Syrah

Tea-Smoked Duck

Gary Chu's Gourmet Chinese Cuisine, Santa Rosa

We like this dish because it has a different flavor from anything else on the menu. We make it twice a week and always run out.
—Gary Chu, chef

1 duck (4 to 5 pounds)
2 tablespoons salt
1 teaspoon Szechwan peppercorns
About ¼ cup uncooked white long-grain rice, or enough to cover bottom of wok
1 stalk fresh sugarcane, sliced in half lengthwise
¼ cup oolong tea leaves

¼ cup orange slices
10 to 12 fresh bamboo shoots, or enough to line steamer
3 star anise pods
1 green onion, including green parts, julienned
2 slices fresh ginger

Rub the duck with the salt and ½ teaspoon of the peppercorns.

Cover the bottom of a wok with a layer of the rice, then the sugarcane, then the tea, and then the orange slices. Place a large steamer in the wok and layer the steamer with the bamboo shoots. Place the duck on top of the bamboo shoots, cover and set over high heat for 8 to 10 minutes, or until the ingredients start to smoke and the duck skin turns brown. Remove the wok from heat. Remove the duck and stuff the body cavity with the star anise, green onion, the remaining ½ teaspoon peppercorns, and the ginger. Steam the duck in a separate wok for 50 to 60 minutes, or until leg or wing bones are showing.

Eat hot, or let cool and refrigerate. To reheat, bake the duck in a preheated 350°F oven for 15 minutes. *Serves 4 as a main course*

Wine-pairing suggestion: Ravenswood Zinfandel

Black-Eyed Peas with Smoked Turkey

Willie Bird Turkeys, Santa Rosa

The Benedetti Family began raising turkeys in Sonoma County over fifty years ago. In 1963, Willie Benedetti developed the formula for the famous Willie Bird turkey, which the family now raises in the rolling oak-studded hills east of Santa Rosa.

2 Willie Bird smoked turkey drumsticks (1 pound each)
3 cups dried black-eyed peas, picked over and rinsed
1 onion
2 garlic cloves
1 bay leaf
3 carrots, peeled and halved crosswise

3 celery stalks, halved crosswise
3 quarts water
1 bunch leafy greens such as kale or Swiss chard, coarsely chopped
1 tablespoon white wine vinegar
1½ tablespoons balsamic vinegar
Salt and freshly ground pepper

Discard the skin and any excess fat from the drumsticks. In a large pot, combine the turkey, black-eyed peas, onion, garlic, bay leaf, carrots, celery, and water. Bring to a boil, then reduce heat to a simmer, and cook for 50 to 55 minutes, or until the peas are tender but not yet falling apart. During cooking, skim off any scum that rises to the top. Strain the liquid through a large sieve. Reserve the liquid. Discard the onion, garlic, and bay leaf, but remove the carrots, celery, and turkey and set them aside to cool.

Return the peas to the pot with about 6 cups of the reserved cooking liquid and the greens. Stir, then bring to a simmer, cover, and cook for 10 to 12 minutes, or until the greens are tender. While the greens cook, remove the meat from the turkey drumsticks and dice it. Dice the carrots and celery.

Add the turkey meat, carrots, and celery to the pot and simmer for 20 to 30 minutes. Remove from heat and stir in the vinegars. Season with salt and generous amounts of pepper. *Serves 12 as a main course*

Wine-pairing suggestion: Arrowood Merlot

CHESTER AARON GARLIC

Chester Aaron grows garlic. Not the plain white supermarket kind, which, he tells you with authority, is 'California Late,' a soft-neck variety with a long shelf life, and a bland taste. Chester grows ninety-some varieties from twenty-five countries, with exotic names like Brown Tempest, Rose du Var, Celaya Purple, and Creole Red.

Chester plants about thirty thousand garlic cloves every year to produce a ton of garlic in the sloping, south-facing pasture next to his Sonoma County home. He grows the different varieties, carefully mapped to mark their identity, in raised beds, with aviary wire bottoms to foil the ever-appreciative gophers. The climate on Chester's hill has a warmth that the little town of Occidental lacks, sited in a valley and surrounded by redwood trees.

Almost single-handedly, Chester has changed the way chefs, food writers, and purveyors think about garlic, much as Robert Mondavi convinced the American people there was more to wine than red or white in one-gallon jugs. Backyard growers who remember an unusual variety from their childhood or homeland have sought out Chester after reading about him in newspapers or magazines, hearing him interviewed on National Public Radio, or finding him on the Internet. Consulted by growers in Russia, Europe, and Asia as well as in America, he now manages an international correspondence, generously giving growing advice, sharing tips, and exchanging garlic lore, all with the goal of ensuring the continued cultivation of heirloom garlic varieties.

His generosity is returned by alliophiles who share treasured memories and varieties with him, selecting the best bulbs brought from their homeland often by grandparents or even great-grandparents. Chester believes that

over the last ten years, as European and Asian ethnic groups have moved across America bringing their cuisines, their garlics have found a home here as well. Chinese garlics, middle-Eastern garlics, African garlics, his collection grows year by year, continent by continent.

Until Chester started growing garlic and swapping the bulbs with his friends, neighbors, and customers in the early nineties, no one thought much about garlic, or knew that the garlic clan is divided into soft-neck types—easy to braid and long lasting—and hard necks, which cannot be braided well and are perishable, lasting only about three or four months. Chester prefers the richer flavors of the hard necks. Although he started growing garlic casually while he lived on a sheep farm, when he chanced on a garlic named after his father's Russian village, he was hooked. As a farmer, Chester stepped into footsteps thousands of years old, for garlic has been documented as one of the oldest cultivated crops, long treasured as a medicinal and a culinary herb.

A member of the genus *Allium* and lily family, garlic is related to chives, onions, shallots, and leeks. The common elephant garlic is actually a member of the leek group and is not a garlic at all. As he began his collection, Chester discovered that garlics, like different grape varieties, have different flavors. Some attack the tongue with peppery sensations, while some fill the mouth with rich, buttery flavors and then a tang far back on the tongue. Some, such as Burgundy, explode in the mouth with a heat that only time diminishes. As his collection and his fame grew, Chester added garlic-related books and a poster to his long list of published novels, children's books, and young-adult novels.

Chester now grows garlic mainly for a list of subscribers, with whom he keeps in close contact through letters and phone calls. Anyone who knows Chester brings him unusual garlics whenever and wherever they stumble across them. His prodigious knowledge of garlic traditions, medicinal and culinary recipes, folklore, and superstitions, has made Chester a Sonoma County legend.

Left and above: Chester Aaron grows over ninety different varieties of garlic. He cultivates them on his little farm in Occidental, hanging them up to dry after harvest in a small shed shaded by redwood trees.
Overleaf: Many of Chester's garlic varieties have exotic names such as (*from left to right, at top*) Simonetti, Pyongyang, Chilote, Chinese Pink, Choparsky, Creole Red, Siberian, Zahroda, French Germindor, Beijing, Bogatyr, Russian Giant, Gigante Morado, Rojo Pais Baza, Music Pink, Volghiera, Transylvanian, and Persian Star.

White Almond–Garlic Soup with Grapes

Chester Aaron Garlic, Occidental

This is my favorite of all garlic soups. It is limited, however, to being offered only in the summer because it must be served chilled. I do not consider it as tasty or distinct when heated. Note: In Spain, grapes or melon balls are often used in cold garlic soups to cut the bite of garlic. Also to cut their bite, peeled garlic cloves are sometimes stored overnight in the refrigerator in milk.
—Chester Aaron, owner, and Thomas Stegmaier, chef

2 cups blanched almonds, ground

3 slices white bread, crusts removed, chopped

10 cloves garlic

6 cups milk

2 teaspoons sherry vinegar

1 cup extra virgin olive oil

Salt and freshly ground pepper

36 seedless green grapes, halved lengthwise,
    for garnish

In a blender, combine the almonds, bread, garlic, milk, and vinegar. Purée until smooth. With the machine running, gradually add the oil. If the mixture tastes too strongly of either garlic or vinegar, add a small amount of water. Add salt and pepper to taste. Refrigerate the soup for at least 2 hours or up to 5 hours. Serve in bowls, garnished with grape halves. *Serves 6 as a first course*

Note: I recommend a hot garlic for this recipe: California Late, Asian Tempest, or German Red. If you like moderately hot garlic, try Duganskij from the Czech Republic. They might be found in local farmer's markets or on the Internet at garlic sites.

Wine-pairing suggestion: Alderbrook Gewürztraminer

Sautéed Hen-of-the-Woods Mushrooms with Pancetta and Greens

Gourmet Mushrooms, Sebastopol

Serve as a side dish or atop polenta. If hen-of-the-woods mushrooms are not available, you can replace them with black trumpet or stemmed shiitake mushrooms.
—Bob Engel, chef

2 tablespoons olive oil

3 ounces pancetta, finely diced (see note)

2 cloves garlic, minced

6 ounces hen-of-the-woods (maitake) mushrooms,
    torn or cut into pieces

1 pound spinach, Swiss chard, broccoli rabe, or
    a mixture of these or other braising greens,
    coarsely chopped

2 tablespoons balsamic vinegar

Salt and freshly ground pepper

Shaved Parmesan cheese for garnish (optional)

In a large skillet, heat the oil over medium heat. Add the pancetta and sauté until it browns lightly. Add the garlic and mushrooms. Sauté for 3 or 4 minutes, then add the greens and cook just until they wilt. Remove from heat immediately and add the balsamic vinegar and salt and pepper to taste. Serve at once, garnished with Parmesan cheese, if you like. *Serves 4 as a side dish*

Note: If you cannot obtain pancetta, substitute 2 strips of thick-sliced bacon, blanched in hot water for 2 minutes and patted dry. Dice the bacon and proceed as above.

Wine-pairing suggestion: Sebastopol Vineyards, Dutton Ranch Pinot Noir

Left: Malcolm Clark of Gourmet Mushrooms, located in Sebastopol, grows a variety of exotic mushrooms from shiitakes to cinnamon caps, pompom blancs, and dozens of others. His mushrooms sell at the local supermarkets and are featured on menus in county restaurants, as well as being shipped to individuals, fine restaurants, and stores all over America.

PORTOBELLO MUSHROOM AND GOAT CHEESE PIZZA

St. Francis Winery Kitchen, Santa Rosa

*Try this recipe for a delicious pizza that is fun to make and very satisfying to eat. As a rule,
I like to serve Zinfandel with Italian foods, and this pizza is no exception. (If you don't want to make
the pizza dough by hand, buy a premade one. I won't tell.)*
—*Todd Muir, chef*

Pizza Dough

1½ cups warm (105° to 115°F) water

1 teaspoon sugar

1 package active dry yeast

3 cups all-purpose flour

1½ cups semolina flour

1 teaspoon salt

1 tablespoon olive oil

Cornmeal for dusting pans

Topping

2 portobello mushrooms, stemmed

2 teaspoons minced garlic

2 tablespoons olive oil, plus more for drizzling

Salt and freshly ground pepper

½ cup tomato sauce

2 cups (16 ounces) shredded mozzarella

1¼ cups (6 ounces) crumbled fresh white
  goat cheese

8 slices prosciutto, cut into wide strips

2 tablespoons minced fresh flat-leaf parsley

2 tablespoons grated Parmesan cheese

For the dough, combine the water, sugar, and yeast in the bowl of a heavy-duty electric mixer. Stir to dissolve the yeast. Let sit for 10 minutes, or until foamy. Add the flours, salt, and oil. Using the dough hook, mix until the dough pulls away from the sides of the bowl. Transfer the dough to a lightly floured board and knead for about 5 minutes, or until smooth and elastic. Place the dough in a lightly oiled large bowl and cover with a clean, dry cloth. Let rise in a warm place for about 1 hour, or until the dough has doubled in size.

While the dough is rising, prepare the marinade for the topping: Combine the portobello mushrooms, garlic, and the 2 tablespoons olive oil in a bowl. Add salt and pepper to taste. Toss to coat. Let sit for 1 hour.

Preheat the oven to 500°F. Put the mushrooms in a small roasting pan and roast in the oven for about 5 minutes, or until tender. Remove from the oven, cut into ¼-inch-thick slices, and set aside.

Punch down the dough. Transfer the dough to a lightly floured board. Roll the dough into a ball and divide into 2 equal pieces. With a rolling pin, roll each piece of dough into a 14-inch round. Place each round on a baking sheet lightly dusted with cornmeal.

Spread each pizza with half of the tomato sauce, then sprinkle evenly with half of the mozzarella, the sliced mushrooms, and goat cheese. Bake for about 8 minutes, or until the cheese has melted. Remove from the oven. Top with the prosciutto and bake for 2 minutes, or until the prosciutto is just warmed through. Remove from the oven, drizzle the crusts with olive oil, and sprinkle the topping with parsley and Parmesan. Cut each pizza into 8 slices and serve.

Makes two 14-inch pizzas; serves 4 as a main course

Wine-pairing suggestion: 1999 St. Francis "Old Vines" Sonoma County Zinfandel

Left and above: The tiny village of Freestone, now an historic district, boasts the only enzyme spa in the country. Osmosis Enzyme Bath and Massage brings a Japanese heat treatment to Sonoma County. Wooden tubs filled with fine shavings of cedar and Douglas fir contain more than six hundred enzymes, which heat up naturally to provide a luxurious waterless soak. A cup of enzyme-laden tea in a peaceful Japanese tea garden sets the tone before the tub, and a blanket wrap or massage ends the experience. The treatment is said to detoxify the body.

Top, above, and right: Spring comes to Sonoma Valley vineyards with the first breaking of the leaf buds on the grapevines. Workers prune the vines during the winter, when they are dormant, a lengthy task needing training and skill.
Overleaf: Vineyards edge the Russian River, growing in soil enriched by countless bouts of flooding over the centuries.

Left, top, and above: Viognier grapes, a Rhône variety, are ready for harvest in the Russian River Valley appellation. The generous harvest of grape clusters is a testament to the painstaking spring and summer pruning that exposes ripening grapes to sunlight and makes harvesting easier. The harvest crews hoist laden bins of grapes into large gondolas that, when full, will be trucked back to the winery for crushing.

Left and above: Hop Kiln Winery, originally a hop farm, preserves the hop kiln's characteristic shape, designed to dry hanging hop vines and flowers. Here, the yellowing leaves of the grapes reflect the end of the harvest year, before the vines go into winter hibernation.

Top: The Russian River Valley appellation includes older wineries, like Korbel Champagne Cellars, established by three Czech brothers who went from lumbering redwood boxes for cigars to planting vineyards and, by 1882, selling wine and brandy. Their sparkling wine is made by the classic *méthode champenoise*.

Overleaf: The long, wet spring in Sonoma County encourages the growth of both pasture hay and sown hay crops, essential to dairies and livestock producers during the five dry months of summer when the brown pastures are barren of any nutrition for cows, sheep, and goats.

BELLWETHER FARMS

The noise level in the barn is deafening, with the low-pitched bleats of the sheep and the higher calls of lambs. Walking by a lambing "jug," the small pen enclosing a mother and her newborn lambs, Cindy Callahan reaches down to find a triplet wedged into a corner. "Hey you, get up and eat." She leans over the low wooden railing to hoist up the baby and nudge it toward its mother's bulging udder. It looks around hungrily and starts to poke at the nipple. The little tail waggles happily as the lamb begins to nurse.

Lawyer, nurse, farmer, cheese maker, and small-business owner, Cindy Callahan attributes her success to her late husband, Ed, who always encouraged her new ventures and backed up her decisions. Originally, they bought sheep to eat down the pastures of the new farm when the Callahans moved to Sonoma County from San Francisco in 1986. Making cheese because she had sheep, Cindy quickly gained a local reputation as the crazy woman from San Francisco who thought sheep could be milked. Sonoma County is dairy country, but until Cindy arrived, *dairy* meant cows, with a few grudgingly accepted goat dairy operations.

Cindy started out with Polypay sheep, a meat sheep bought from her neighbors up the road. She started her business by selling baby lamb to restaurants in San Francisco. She discovered sheep's milk cheese when a Syrian friend described sheep's milk yogurt to her. Eventually, she changed her flock to East Friesian sheep, a European milking variety. Cindy admits she blundered a bit learning how to make the cheese; then in 1992 she and Ed went to Italy with the names of sheep cheese producers, courtesy of the noted author Carol Field. Cindy brought home new ideas for her cheeses. By this time, her sons had become involved in the dairy, and in 1994 she sent Liam, her eldest, to Italy to study cheese making as well. That year, Bellwether received its first national award for one of its sheep's milk cheeses.

Sheep produce small quantities of milk, however, and at best, only eight months a year. In a family conference, it was decided to send Liam and his wife, Diana, back to Europe to study cow's milk cheeses. Today Bellwether Farm produces a range of cow's milk cheeses made from ultra-fat Jersey milk purchased from a neighbor. They now make cow's milk cheeses all year long, adding sheep's milk cheeses after lambing. They have made it a family business, with Liam Callahan the cheese maker; his wife, Diana, handling orders; and brother, Brett Callahan, the liaison with the Bay Area restaurants for deliveries, and daily collecting the milk and cream for the cow's milk cheeses. Brett also works with Cindy to care for the sheep and make sure they are healthy for milking and lambing.

Perched high up on the crest of a hill halfway between Petaluma and Bodega Harbor, the barn smells of sweet milk, with a tangy hint of fermentation. Everywhere, stainless-steel sinks, vats, and tables gleam. Along one side of the cheese-making room, huge doors open to the aging rooms, with wooden shelves filled with neat rows of cheese, one room for sheep cheese, one for cow.

The sheep's milk cheeses are made from unpasteurized milk, while the cow's milk is pasteurized. Every step of the cheese-making process is done by hand, with Liam stirring the cultures into the warm milk, hand cutting the developing curds into neat squares in buckets, then pouring the curds into forms to drain and be salted or brined, depending on the cheese.

During sheep-milking time, the flock of 150 sheep is milked twice a day and the milk is made into cheeses that are aged for two months. At the same time, Liam makes both fresh cheeses and aged cheeses from cow's milk. The daily work is unending, from the careful tending of the dairy animals to the making and nurturing of the cheeses, to the packaging and selling. A new line of fresh cow's milk cheeses—ricotta, crème fraîche, and fromage blanc—has added more variety to Bellwether's cheeses.

Bellwether Farms cheeses are found in stores and restaurants all over America, from Bizou in San Francisco to the famed Murray's Cheese Shop in New York City. The family celebrates the age-old tradition of hand work with each cheese, and sees themselves as stewards of a process that starts from sheep and ends with a bite of richly perfumed cheese.

Left and above: East Friesian sheep leave the milking parlor at Bellwether Farms. The Callahan family maintains the dairy, produces and markets both their cow and sheep's milk cheeses, and sells fresh young lamb in the spring. The Callahan's, *above, from left,* Cindy, Brett, Liam, Diana, and grandson Connor.

Top, above, and right: The Callahan family values the East Friesian sheep that are milked twice a day for seven to eight months a year. Cindy and a dairy helper pour fresh sheep's milk into a large vat ready for the addition of cheese-making cultures. Later, Liam fills cheese forms with developed curds ready to be brined and drained. The reward for all their hard work lies in the rows of aging sheep's milk cheeses.

Left: The village of Bodega lies just a few miles inland from Bodega Harbor surrounded by nearby goat, sheep, and cow dairies. Pastures near Bodega are kept green by summer fog, making them prime grazing areas. Situated on a hill in the center of town, St. Theresa's Catholic Church is a turn-of-the-century, local landmark. To the rear of the church stands another historic landmark— the Potter schoolhouse—the site of the famous school yard "crow" scene in Alfred Hitchcock's 1963 classic thriller, "The Birds," which was filmed chiefly in the town and coastal area of Bodega Bay.

Top and above: Four miles west of Bodega is Bodega Bay, discovered in 1775 by the Spanish explorer Juan Francisco de la Bodega y Cuadra. The harbor began as a small fishing village, but now boasts a golf course as well as a number of seafood restaurants that cook up the haul from the local fishing fleet. During the season, visitors arrive from all over the Bay Area to buy live crabs or to picnic on cooked crabs at the Pacific beaches nearby.

Dungeness Crab Cakes with Tomato–Ginger Chutney

The Duck Club Restaurant, Bodega Bay

I've had this on our menu for eight years. If I took it off, people would scream. What's not to like? —*Jeffrey Reilly, chef*

1 pound fresh lump Dungeness crabmeat,
  picked over for shell
1 stalk celery, finely diced
¼ red onion, finely diced
Grated zest and juice of 1 lemon
Grated zest and juice of ½ lime
½ teaspoon ground cumin

2 egg yolks
⅓ cup mayonnaise
2 tablespoons chopped fresh cilantro
Tabasco sauce to taste
¼ cup panko (Japanese bread crumbs)
2 tablespoons canola oil
Tomato-Ginger Chutney (recipe follows)

Combine all the ingredients except the panko and oil in a bowl and stir to blend. Form into ¼-cup patties and coat with the panko. In a large sauté pan or skillet, heat the oil over medium-high heat and sauté the patties for about 1½ minutes on each side, or until golden brown. Serve with the chutney alongside. *Serves 4 as a first course*

Wine-pairing suggestion: Murphy Goode Reserve Fumé Blanc

Tomato–Ginger Chutney

6 pounds tomatoes, peeled, diced, and drained
2 tablespoons minced garlic
3 tablespoons grated fresh ginger
2 teaspoons red pepper flakes
⅔ cup sugar
2 cups apple cider vinegar
2 teaspoons ground cumin
2 teaspoons kosher salt
Leaves from ⅓ bunch cilantro, chopped

Combine the tomatoes, garlic, ginger, and red pepper flakes in a large nonreactive saucepan. Stir to blend. Bring to a simmer over medium heat and cook for 10 minutes, or until almost dry. Stir in the sugar, vinegar, cumin, and salt. Cook for about 45 minutes, stirring constantly. Add the cilantro and simmer for 2 minutes. Remove from heat and let cool. Use immediately, or cover and refrigerate for up to 1 month. *Makes 4 cups*

Above and right: Dungeness crabs are large—two to three pounds—and filled with sweet succulent meat. The crab fisherman in their large boats often must collect their crab pots in heavy seas and cold and rainy winter weather. The work is dangerous, and every contented crab eater owes them thanks.

Mama's Paella

Kozlowski Farms, Forestville

This recipe originated in Southern Spain in the town of Archez, in the mountain region near Malagá along the Costa del Sol. My grandmother, Julia Martin Lorenzo, whom we called Mama, brought this recipe with her to the States when she emigrated in 1919. Her cooking brought our families together and taught us a love of good food.
—*Carol Kozlowski-Every, co-owner*

½ cup Spanish olive oil (Borgus or Star Brand)

3 boneless skin-on chicken breasts, each cut in half crosswise

3 boneless center-cut pork chops, each cut in half crosswise

2 Spanish chorizo sausages, cut into 1-inch-thick diagonal pieces

1 large yellow onion, finely chopped

16-ounce jar Kozlowski Farms Salsa de Lorenzo

1 teaspoon salt

¼ teaspoon freshly ground pepper

2 cups long-grain white rice

3 cups water

1 cup dry white wine

1½ cups canned low-sodium chicken broth

1 tablespoon Kozlowski Farms Red Raspberry Vinegar

1 small red bell pepper, seeded, deribbed, and chopped

8 ounces frozen small peas

8 ounces frozen artichoke hearts, each halved lengthwise

8 ounces bay scallops

8 ounces calamari, cleaned and cut into 1-inch tubes

3 cloves garlic, crushed

¼ teaspoon Spanish saffron threads

1 pound clams, scrubbed

1 pound mussels, scrubbed and debearded

8 ounces medium shrimp in the shell

12 asparagus tips, steamed, for garnish (optional)

1 jar pimiento strips for garnish (optional)

Preheat the oven to 375°F. Heat ¼ cup of the olive oil over medium-high heat in a large, ovenproof skillet or paella pan. Add the chicken and brown on all sides. Using tongs, transfer the chicken to a plate and cover to keep warm. Repeat with the pork, then the chorizo, transferring the chorizo to paper towels to drain.

Clean the skillet. Heat the remaining ¼ cup olive oil over medium heat and cook the onion for about 3 minutes, or until translucent. Add the Salsa de Lorenzo, salt, and pepper, and cook for 5 minutes. Add the rice, 2 cups of the water, wine, chicken broth, vinegar, and bell pepper. Cover and cook for 20 minutes. Add the peas, artichoke hearts, scallops, calamari, garlic, and saffron. Fold all the ingredients together.

Place the pan in the oven and bake for 20 minutes, or until almost all the liquid has been absorbed.

A few minutes before the rice is cooked, put the clams and mussels in a heavy pot with the remaining 1 cup water. Bring to a boil and cook for 2 minutes. Add the shrimp, cover, and cook for 2 minutes longer, or until the clams and mussels open. Remove from heat. Discard any clams or mussels that have not opened.

Remove the paella from the oven, leaving the oven on. Arrange the clams, mussels, asparagus, and pimientos on top. Return the paella to the oven for about 10 minutes, or until heated through. *Serves 6 to 8 as a main course*

Wine-pairing suggestion: Sebastopol Vineyards Dutton Ranch Chardonnay or Pinot Noir

Kasu Sake Salmon

Feast, American Bistro, Santa Rosa

This dish gives you an opportunity to use some ingredients that might be new to you, but that are readily available. I always put this dish on the menu when salmon season opens on the Sonoma Coast.
—Jesse McQuarrie, chef

Kasu Marinade

¾ cup mirin, available in the Asian section of
   most grocery stores
¼ cup rice vinegar
½ cup sugar
¾ cup light soy sauce (preferably Kikkoman brand)
1½ cups kasu (see note)

One 3-pound salmon fillet
Kosher salt

Sweet Shoyu Sauce

3 cups water
3 cups rice vinegar
2 cups light soy sauce
2 cups sugar
2 tablespoons ebi furikake (see note)
¼ teaspoon white truffle oil
3 tablespoons cornstarch mixed with 3 tablespoons
   water

Steamed spinach, grated daikon, and Meyer lemon
   wedges for serving

Preheat the broiler. For the marinade, combine all the ingredients except the kasu in a saucepan. Pour into a blender. Add the kasu and blend together until well blended. Spread a liberal layer of marinade over the salmon and season with salt to taste. Place on a broiler pan and broil for 10 to 12 minutes, or until slightly caramelized.

Meanwhile, make the sauce: In a nonreactive saucepan, combine all the ingredients except the cornstarch mixture. Bring to a boil, then whisk in the cornstarch mixture and continue whisking for 1 minute, or until thickened. Immediately remove from heat.

Cut the salmon into fillets and serve with the shoyu sauce and steamed spinach, grated daikon, and Meyer lemon wedges on the side. *Serves 6 to 8 as a main course*

Note: Kasu is the leftover yeast fermentation at the bottom of the sake barrels. You can find it at Asian markets. Furikake is a Japanese spice, also available at Asian markets.

Wine-pairing suggestion: Mayo Viognier

NORTH COAST KING SALMON
WITH MEYER LEMON AND CHANTERELLE SAUCE

MIXX Restaurant, Santa Rosa

We have the best mushroom forager around, so when mushrooms are in season and local salmon
is available, this is a hard combination to beat. —Dan Berman, chef

1 tablespoon peanut or canola oil

2 king salmon fillets (6 ounces each)

Flour for coating, seasoned with salt and
   freshly ground pepper

1 tablespoon unsalted butter

4 ounces chanterelles or morels, sliced

½ teaspoon minced garlic

½ teaspoon minced shallot

¼ cup Chardonnay wine

¼ cup fish stock or light chicken stock

½ cup heavy whipping cream

Grated zest of 1 Meyer lemon

1 tablespoon freshly squeezed Meyer lemon juice

1 teaspoon minced fresh flat-leaf parsley

Salt and freshly ground pepper

4 fresh basil leaves, stacked, rolled, and cut into
   fine shreds

Heat the oil in a large sauté pan or skillet over medium-high heat until almost smoking. Lightly dredge the fish in the seasoned flour. Gently shake off the excess flour. Place the fish in the pan and sauté on each side for about 2 minutes, or until golden. Transfer to a plate, cover, and keep warm.

Pour the excess oil out of the pan. Add the butter and melt over medium heat until it foams. Add the mushrooms and sauté until they release their juice. Add the garlic and shallot and sauté for 1 to 2 minutes, or until the shallot is translucent. Add the Chardonnay, bring to a boil, and cook to reduce by half, about 2 minutes. Repeat with the fish stock. Add the cream, boil, and cook to reduce until slightly thickened. Add the lemon zest, lemon juice, parsley, and salt and pepper to taste. Place 1 fillet on each of 2 warmed plates. Divide the sauce evenly in a diagonal fashion over the fish. Sprinkle with the basil and serve. *Serves 2 as a main course*

Wine-pairing suggestion: 2000 J. Rochioli, River Block Estate Chardonnay, Russian River Valley

ASIAN MARINATED SKEWERED CALIFORNIA ALBACORE
WRAPPED IN BACON

The Tides Wharf & Restaurant, Bodega Bay

I use this great recipe during the summer when I can get albacore from our local fishing boats. —Ken Schloss, executive chef

1 pound California albacore tuna, cut into
   sixteen 1-inch cubes

16 slices bacon

Asian Marinade

1 tablespoon red chile paste

5 cloves garlic, minced

1 tablespoon minced fresh ginger

2 tablespoons chopped fresh cilantro

5 tablespoons soy sauce

1 teaspoon canola oil

Soak 4 bamboo skewers in water for 1 hour to prevent burning during grilling. Wrap each albacore cube with a slice of bacon and thread on the skewers.

For the marinade, combine all the ingredients in a baking dish just large enough to hold the skewers. Stir to blend. Add the skewers and marinate for at least 1 hour or up to 24 hours, turning occasionally.

Prepare a fire in a charcoal grill or preheat a gas grill to high. Place the skewers on the grill and cook for about 6 minutes, turning occasionally, or until the fish turns opaque. *Serves 4 as a main course*

Wine-pairing suggestion: Ravenswood Monte Rosso Zinfandel

Right: North Coast King Salmon with Meyer Lemon and Chanterelle Sauce.

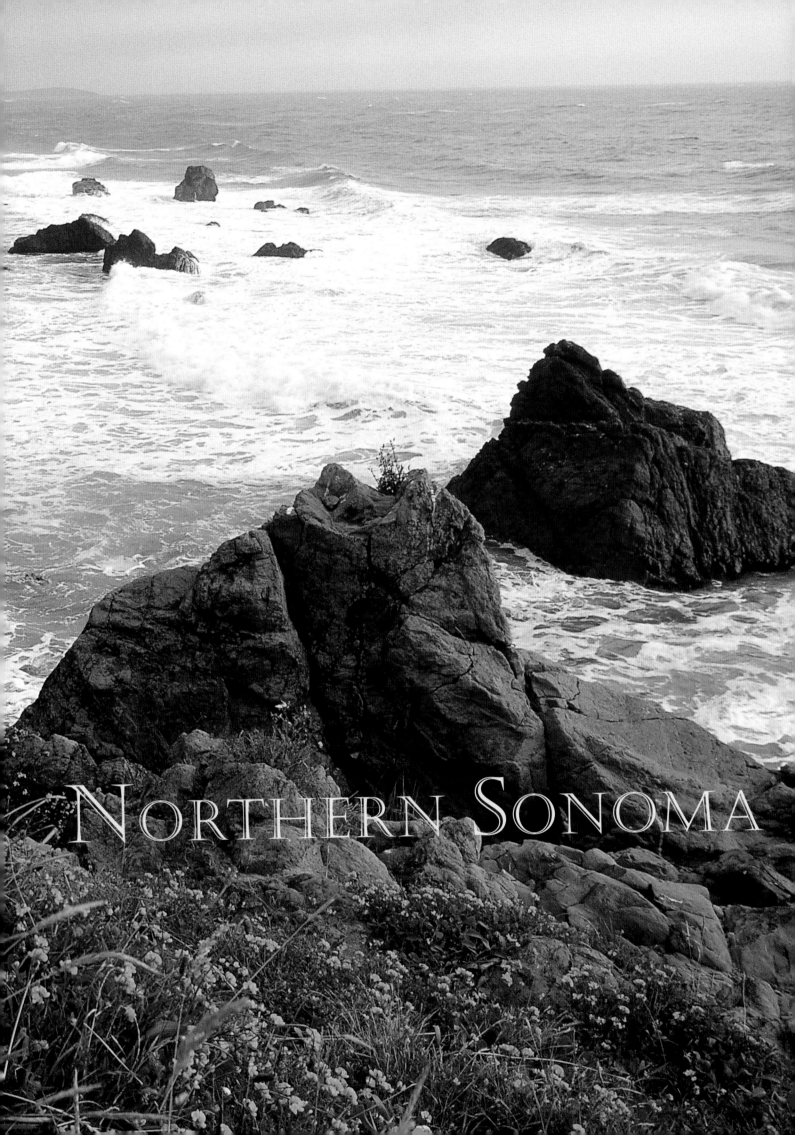

NORTHERN SONOMA

Northern Sonoma

The northern end of Sonoma Valley, buffered from the coast by the barrier of western coastal hills, simmers with summer heat that edges up into the nineties during the daytime and stays warm at night, often in the seventies. Cloverdale, the northernmost town, was established in 1859 by James Kleiser, an olive-oil producer who worked to connect his town to the railroad that ran north from Petaluma. The transportation of north county agricultural and timber products depended on the train to Petaluma and the boats to San Francisco.

The Russian River, with its headwaters far to the north in Mendocino County, winds past Cloverdale and along the edge of Healdsburg, a small town with a Spanish-style grassy, tree-shaded plaza. Below Healdsburg, the river runs southwest to its ocean outlet at Jenner. Sandwiched between Eastside and Westside Roads, its slow-moving waters irrigate the vineyards of the Russian River Valley appellation. The shimmering heat of summer days brings swimmers to the river and its sandy beaches.

The enveloping summer heat of the appellations of Dry Creek Valley, Alexander Valley, and Knights Valley is barely mitigated by rare touches of fog. Dry Creek Valley, north and west of Healdsburg, just two miles wide and sixteen miles long, grows Sauvignon Blanc and Chardonnay grapes in the rich red soil. The warmer hillsides encourage heat-loving Zinfandel, Cabernet Sauvignon, and Merlot grapes. To the east of the Russian River, Alexander Valley, twenty miles long, was originally settled in the mid-1800s by Cyrus Alexander of Pennsylvania. For years the lush valley was used for grazing beef cattle, but Alexander Valley now boasts a widening range of grape varieties, including the newly introduced Viognier and Sangiovese. The Knights Valley appellation, just to the southeast, is the warmest in the county.

Olive trees soak up the heat of this Mediterranean climate. Just behind Westside Road, ranks of trees climb the hills belonging to Olive Ridge, producers of DaVero Extra Virgin Olive Oil. The summer heat also ripens peaches, tomatoes, pumpkins, and peppers. Small farms patched in between the vineyards sell their products at the Healdsburg farmers' market as well as the other county markets. Dry Creek Peach and Produce, with one thousand bearing trees, grows more than thirty varieties of peaches such as Rich May and Suncrest. The chin-dripping fruit is hand-picked ripe, not green, and is coddled to reach the marketplace with flavor developed to ambrosia and its flesh unbruised.

Preceding pages: Sonoma County's beauty includes the meeting of land and ocean, and its craggy rocks, cliffs, and stretches of beaches are stunning.
Left and above: Fort Ross, the Russian settlement that predated the Spanish arrival in Sonoma County, has been restored and re-created as a California State Historic Park. The second-growth redwoods growing along the coast give a hint of what the thickly covered hills might have looked like to the early explorers and settlers.

Left: The Russian River, flowing down from Mendocino County to empty into the Pacific Coast at the town of Jenner, supplies the water to irrigate grapes and other crops of northern Sonoma, as well as to provide recreational opportunities for swimming, canoeing, and fishing.

Top and above: The Healdsburg town square is ringed with restaurants, bakeries, bookstores, wine shops, and fine delicatessens. Downtown Bakery & Creamery, owned by famed former Chez Panisse pastry chef Lindsey Shere, makes a pleasant morning stop for coffee and fine pastries. House-made breads and jams are also sold there.

Top: Jimtown Store, at the top of Alexander Valley, combines a small grocery with freshly baked snacks and lunchtime soups and sandwiches. Antiques and bed and bath items are also for sale in this one-of-a-kind store.

Above and right: You can pick up supplies for a picnic lunch at Raymond Burr Vineyards in Dry Creek Valley, just a short drive west from Geyserville. Vines planted during the actor's lifetime have matured to produce award-winning vintages.

DaVero Extra Virgin Olive Oil

Twenty acres of olive trees climb the steep hill behind the house that was supposed to be just a weekend country escape from cold San Francisco summers. Ridgely Evers admits that he thought he was going to relax in the country, a respite from his intense world of computer technology, and for a couple of years it worked, and his grassy east-facing hillsides lay fallow. Then, as he puts it, he got the "ag bug."

Now those empty fields are closely planted with forty-five hundred olive trees. They produce up to fifteen hundred cases of extra virgin olive oil in a good year. Although the crop tonnage varies depending on the weather, it should increase as the trees mature into full production. DaVero lies outside the inland town of Healdsburg, some eighty miles north of San Francisco. Protected from the summer coastal fog, the temperatures rise to the high eighties during the day and drop down to the sixties most evenings—a Tuscan climate.

When he decided to become an agriculturalist, Ridgely admits he considered following his neighbors' example and planting wine grapes, but that year was a bad one for grapes and prices plummeted, so he decided on olives instead. Loving everything Italian, he went to Tuscany and tasted olive oil until he found one he liked, from Fattoria Mansi Bernardini, a 350-year-old farm east of Lucca. He drove out to the estate, met the owners, and ended up with cuttings of their trees, with the varieties Leccino, Frantoio, Maurino, and Pendolino. After getting through agricultural inspections and quarantine, the diminutive olive trees were nurtured, further propagated, and planted out on those empty hillsides. Unlike many olive growers in California, Ridgely follows the Italian tradition of field planting, setting out different varieties of trees intermixed in the rows. Most olive producers separate the varieties, crush them separately, and then blend the different oils. DaVero's olives are all harvested and crushed together.

Ridgely has the help of Colleen McGlynn, his wife and co-producer, who is also a professional chef. They work together to develop the DaVero products, including a lemon olive oil and a blended virgin olive oil for restaurant kitchens. Colleen also picks up all the loose ends of the business, from driving out to the valley to bring home a new ten-thousand gallon

Left and above: Colleen McGlynn and Ridgely Evers are the husband-and-wife producers of estate-grown DaVero extra virgin olive oil. As small-business partners, they do everything from organizing the picking teams to ordering and filling bottles and attending culinary events and tastings.

stainless-steel tank for storing pressed oil, to staffing the shipping department (a one-person department, she remarks), marketing the product to local stores, and supervising tastings at white-tablecloth culinary events.

Even though olive oil sales in America have increased due to the recognition of its healthful advantages and an increased appreciation of its flavor, most Americans are confused about the definition of extra virgin olive oil. The range of prices in the marketplace, from the dirt-cheap European varieties to the premium California types, adds to the confusion. "Extra virgin" is an awkward translation from the Italian, which simply means "first class." In the United States, there is no legal definition of "virgin olive oil," and Ridgely moans that you can legally put an extra virgin olive oil label on motor oil and not be disputed. DaVero submits its oil to national judgings that designate standards for virgin olive oil in America, and has recently received the top gold in a Los Angeles competition.

Creating such a superb product means tireless attention to detail. Olives must be harvested from the tree, for if they are picked fallen from the ground, they will add a bitter flavor to the oil. As soon as they are picked, the olives must be taken to the press. DaVero uses a stone wheel press in Mill Valley, California, which first grinds the olives then, when the grindings are put into sandwiches of felt layers, presses them out, a process more painstaking than that of the new hydraulic presses that press in one step. But Ridgely and Colleen feel the flavor of their oil justifies the expense.

In the future, there will be a few more DaVero products, all sold like the oils, by word of mouth or through their website. A mixed field planting of Italian wine grape varieties will soon go into the land above the olive orchards. A new planting of Meyer lemons on a sunny slope will provide citrus for the lemon oil. Gradually, the Healdsburg "retreat" is becoming more and more a producing estate, much like the Italian ones Ridgely so admires.

Every year, after the olive harvest in November, Ridgely and Colleen prepare an elegant lunch for their friends, with oven-baked Italian-style breads, platters piled high with vegetables from their garden and locally grown meats, and carafes of their dark green rich olive oil placed every couple of feet down the long tables. Ridgely always starts his welcome speech with the heartfelt phrase, "This is my favorite day of the year."

Left, top, and above: Italians and Spanish immigrants brought olive trees from their Mediterranean homes to California, and the huge-trunked old trees can still be seen gracing hillsides throughout Sonoma County. Today, the county's chefs add sparkle to their dishes with glistening drops of carefully crafted DaVero extra virgin olive oil.

Lamb Stew with Lemons and Olives

Santi, Geyserville

Serve with couscous, rice, or bulgur wheat.
—Thomas Oden, chef, and Bruce H. Campbell, C. K. Lamb

Leaves from 6 sprigs *each* cilantro and flat-leaf
   parsley, minced
1 large onion, grated
3 cloves garlic, minced
Salt and freshly ground pepper
2 pounds C. K. lamb shoulder, cut into 1-inch cubes
¼ cup extra virgin olive oil
1 teaspoon tomato paste
½ lemon, quartered, salted overnight, drained,
   and thinly sliced
1 pound cracked green olives, soaked overnight
   in water, drained
2 cups water

Make a paste of the herbs, onion, garlic, and salt and pepper to taste. Rub the paste on the meat. In a Dutch oven, heat the oil over low heat. Add the meat and all the remaining ingredients. Bring to a boil over medium-high heat, cover, and cook for 10 minutes. Lower the heat to a simmer and cook, partially covered, for 45 minutes, or until the meat is tender and the liquid has thickened. *Serves 6 as a main course*

Wine-pairing suggestion: Limerick Lane Zinfandel

Sonoma County Free-Range Chicken Roasted in Moroccan Spices

Applewood Inn & Restaurant, Guerneville

A great way to serve these juicy birds is with lots of Meyer lemon wedges, a large bowl of green olives,
and extra virgin olive oil for drizzling.
—Brian Gerritsen, chef

½ teaspoon ground cinnamon
½ tablespoon fennel seed
1 tablespoon coriander seed
⅛ teaspoon red pepper flakes
1 teaspoon black peppercorns
½ cup extra virgin olive oil
1 tablespoon chopped garlic
1 tablespoon minced fresh marjoram,
   plus 6 marjoram sprigs
2 Sonoma County Rocky Jr. roasting chickens
   (3 pounds each)
Kosher salt for sprinkling

Preheat the oven to 350°F. Prepare 1 large or 2 medium roasting pans with rack inserts.

In a spice grinder, combine the cinnamon, fennel seed, coriander seed, pepper flakes, and peppercorns. Grind to a fine powder. In a small bowl, combine the spices, olive oil, garlic, and minced marjoram.

Rinse and pat the chickens dry. Salt the cavities generously and place 3 sprigs of marjoram in each. Truss the birds with kitchen twine or simply tie the legs together snugly. Sprinkle the birds with a very generous amount of salt on all sides.

Using your hands, rub the spice mixture over all the birds. Place them in the roasting racks, breast side up. Roast for exactly 30 minutes. Turn the chickens over onto their breasts and roast for an additional 30 minutes. Turn them breast side up again and roast for 30 more minutes. Remove from the oven and let rest for 15 minutes before carving and serving. *Serves 6 to 8 as a main course*

Wine-pairing suggestion: Iron Horse Viognier

Stuffed Chicken Breasts with Ragù of Mushrooms, Jerusalem Artichokes, and Olives

Redwood Hill Farm, Sebastopol

Made by a small family farm that has been producing award-winning cheeses for more than twenty years, Redwood Hill cheese is a staple for chefs and is found on the menus of some of the best restaurants in the country.
—John Ash, chef consultant

4 large boneless chicken breast halves, skin on
(6 to 8 ounces each)

½ cup (4 ounces) Redwood Hill Farm goat cheese
at room temperature

2 teaspoons *each* minced fresh tarragon, mint,
parsley, and chives

1 teaspoon finely grated lemon zest

Salt and freshly ground pepper

6 tablespoons unsalted butter

6 ounces Jerusalem artichokes (sunchokes), peeled
and cut into thick matchsticks

4 tablespoons olive oil

8 ounces cremini or shiitake mushrooms, quartered
(stem shiitakes, if using)

2 tablespoons pitted and finely diced black olives
(such as niçoise)

1 tablespoon minced fresh flat-leaf parsley

1¼ cups rich chicken stock

¼ cup dry white wine

2 tablespoons fresh lemon juice

Cut a 3-inch horizontal pocket in the thickest part of each breast. In a small bowl, combine the goat cheese, herbs, zest, and salt and pepper to taste. Stir to blend. Stuff each breast with one-fourth of the filling and close the pocket with a toothpick. Season the breasts with salt and pepper. Cover and refrigerate while making the ragù.

For the ragù, melt 2 tablespoons of the butter over medium-high heat in a sauté pan or skillet. Add the artichokes and sauté for about 1 minute, or until lightly browned. Using a slotted spoon, transfer to a bowl. Clean the pan and melt 2 tablespoons of the butter with 2 tablespoons of the olive oil over medium heat. Add the mushrooms and sauté until lightly browned. Add the mushrooms to the artichokes. Add the olives and parsley to the mixture. Stir to blend and set aside.

In a large sauté pan or skillet, melt the remaining 2 tablespoons butter with the remaining 2 tablespoons olive oil over medium-high heat. Place the breasts, skin side down, in the pan. Sauté for 5 minutes, or until the skin is golden brown and crisp. Turn and cook for 4 to 5 minutes on the second side, or until opaque throughout and firm to the touch.

Using a slotted metal spatula, transfer the breasts to a plate. Cover and keep warm. Pour the fat from the pan. Place the pan over high heat and add the stock, wine, and lemon juice. Bring to a boil, scraping up any browned bits on the bottom of the pan. Cook to reduce until slightly thickened. Add the ragù, taste for salt and pepper, and heat through. Place the breasts on warmed plates, top with the ragù, and serve immediately. *Serves 4 as a main course*

Wine-pairing suggestion: 2000 Matanzas Creek Sauvignon Blanc

Orange, Almond, and Olive Oil Cake

DaVero Extra Virgin Olive Oil, Healdsburg

I usually make this cake when the weather starts to turn cold. If it doesn't get eaten right away, it will stay moist for days. —Colleen McGlynn, co-owner

2 small oranges
1 lemon
1 cup all-purpose flour
1 tablespoon baking powder
4 eggs at room temperature
½ teaspoon salt

1½ cups sugar
1½ cups (6 ounces) almonds, toasted and finely chopped
⅔ cup olive oil
Confectioners' sugar for dusting

Put the oranges and lemons in a large saucepan and add water to cover. Bring to a simmer and cook, uncovered, for 30 minutes. Drain and let cool to the touch. Cut the lemon in half and discard the pulp and seeds. Cut the oranges in half and discard the seeds, but not the pulp. Put the lemon rind and the orange halves in a food processor and chop finely. Set aside.

Preheat the oven to 350°F. Sift the flour and the baking powder together into a bowl and set aside. In a large bowl, combine the eggs and salt. Beat until foamy. Gradually beat in the sugar. Gently fold in the flour mixture. Stir in the chopped fruit, almonds, and olive oil just until incorporated. Do not overmix.

Pour the batter into a 10-inch springform pan. Bake for about 1 hour and 15 minutes, or until the center of the cake is set or until a toothpick inserted in the center comes out clean. Let cool completely in the pan on a wire rack, then unmold. Place on a serving plate and dust the top with confectioners' sugar. *Makes one 10-inch cake; serves 8*

Wine-pairing suggestion: Iron Horse Brut sparkling wine

Middleton Farm Peach and Blackberry Crisp

Mixx Restaurant, Santa Rosa

Middleton Farm is a six-acre organic farm in Healdsburg run by owner Nancy Skall. Nancy grows several varieties of delicious peaches including Red Haven and Forty-Niner varieties. —Kathleen Berman, pastry chef

6 to 8 large Middleton Farm peaches, peeled, pitted, and cut into large pieces
1¼ cups granulated sugar
1 tablespoon cornstarch
2 cups fresh Middleton Farm blackberries

Streusel Topping
1 cup firmly packed dark brown sugar
⅞ cup granulated sugar
1¼ pound (5 sticks) unsalted butter, chilled
1½ teaspoons vanilla extract
2½ tablespoons ground cinnamon
1 teaspoon salt
2¾ cups all-purpose flour

Preheat the oven to 350°F. Put the peach pieces in a large saucepan. In a bowl, combine the sugar and cornstarch. Whisk to blend. Sift the mixture through a sieve into the saucepan with the peaches. Heat over medium flame for a couple of minutes, stirring with a rubber spatula just until the sugar dissolves. Spoon into individual ramekins equally disperse blackberries among the peaches.

For the topping, cream the sugars, butter, and vanilla together in a heavy-duty mixer fitted with a paddle. Sift the dry ingredients together in a bowl and add to the butter mixture all at once while mixer is off. Mix until combined. Do not overmix or the topping will clump together. Mixture should be crumbly and uniform in color.

Cover the fruit with the streusel topping using a spoon. Place the ramekins on a baking sheet. Bake for 20 to 25 minutes, or until the topping is light brown and the filling is bubbling. *Makes 6 to 8 individual desserts*

Wine-pairing suggestion: Kendall-Jackson 2000 Select Late Harvest Chardonnay

Right: Orange, Almond, and Olive Oil Cake

Left: The Healdsburg farmers' market reflects the diversity of produce grown in the county, such as this crop of peaches from Dry Creek Peach and Produce. *Above:* A trip to the Healdsburg farmers' market will amaze anyone with the abundance of potatoes available in a range of colors, shapes, and sizes. Because potatoes are easily grown in Sonoma County, freshly dug varieties are available almost year-round.

TIERRA VEGETABLES

Lee James is finishing up work in her greenhouse at the end of May, repotting the last of the tomatoes to be planted at the main growing field on Pleasant Road in Windsor, a little town halfway between Santa Rosa and Healdsburg. A small cage hung up in a shady spot holds a bright blue parakeet called Chip, redeemed as a raffle prize and famed for his verbalizations, especially the phrase "Chip wants a chile."

Tierra Vegetables has been growing chiles and other vegetables in Sonoma County for twenty years. The partnership of Lee, her brother Wayne, and her sister-in-law, Evie, is renowned for its fresh chiles, wood-oven-smoked chipotles, chile powder, and potent chile jam. When the ground warms up in May, they set out six thousand plants with names like Eclipse; Sunrise; chilaca (known as pasilla when dried); mulatto, which turns a chocolaty brown when mature; chilhuacle, which is dried for mole; habenero; and the tongue-tingling Scotch Bonnet. From September to Thanksgiving, a staggering 20,000 pounds of chiles are harvested. About 10,000 pounds are oven-roasted chipotles.

During the 1970s, Wayne was in viticulture school, but he spent his summers helping a family friend farm in Potter Valley, north of Santa Rosa. Together they worked forty acres of corn and melons, and the experience made Wayne switch from viticulture to vegetable production. He wanted to grow good, healthful food for people. In his early days, on his own land, he did everything by hand, and he says with a smile that in the first years, he figures he seeded at least a mile of vegetables by hand, on his knees.

The current farm is a two-acre square of flat land, filled in the spring with mounded soil rows loaded with lettuce, garlic, carrots, and onions, all ready to be picked. In the back of the field reside the newly planted tomatoes

and chiles, heralding the start of the summer season. Tierra is currently expanding to property leased from the Sonoma County Open Space District, an exciting partnership between the community and farmers to preserve agriculture in a county fast becoming a suburb of San Francisco.

Wayne, Lee, and Evie have worked for years to build up fertile soil for their almost year-round production schedule. A landscape company mowing twenty-seven acres of lawn in a nearby gated community delivers mountains of grass clippings for compost, making the soil rich enough to turn out buckets of tomatoes, onions, corn, beets, lettuce, and chiles. In addition to selling at farmers' markets in San Francisco, Marin Civic Center, and Healdsburg, Tierra also operates as a CSA, a community-supported agriculture venture, providing weekly boxes of fresh produce to forty to eighty families from June to Thanksgiving. On their website, www.tierravegetables.com, they sell dried chiles, chile powder, and hot chile jam, with its sweet stinging bite, all over America.

Their chipotle production began after a customer at a farmers' market asked whether they had any for sale. Wayne and Lee were intrigued and began to research, discovering that the smoked chiles were a style of Mexican cuisine. Rigging an old refrigerator as a smoker got them started, but they have now upgraded to a wood-fired oven hand-built by Wayne. Using grapevines or fruitwood for the aromatic smoke, they roast about three hundred pounds of ripe red jalapeño chiles at a time, as well as a less conventional but equally delicious mixture of other chiles. When the chiles are ripe in the field in late September, the oven roasts all day and night. It takes a lot of smoke to dry ten thousand pounds of chiles.

The Jameses plan to open a farm stand on their new open-space land, and they may try to cut down to just one day of farmers' markets. Everyone now works seven days a week, with a rare day off for a picnic trip to the beach. But it's clear to the family, they will always be farming, regardless of the long hours and the hard physical work. Wayne, now in his fifties, figures he has at least another thirty years to farm, and Lee agrees. They don't plan on retiring, ever, but plan to keep growing delicious things that are good for people to eat, and to keep the oven smoking chiles.

Left and above: Brother and sister Wayne and Lee James have guru status among Sonoma County farmers because of the rainbow variety of their home-grown chiles. They sell at farmers' markets, to their subscription Community Supported Agriculture (CSA) members, and on the Internet. CSA members prepay for a full season of vegetables, enabling the Jameses to deliver a weekly supply of vegetables fresh from their farm near the town of Windsor.

Ever vigilant for new varieties, Wayne has collected chile seeds in Mexico, and tries new types every year. His chipotle chiles are sold whole or ground to add their smoky heat to chili and other dishes.

Above, top, and right: Although the spring planting of chiles looks like a field of tiny sticks, come the warm days of summer, the bushes are laden with green chiles that ripen to colors ranging from red to orange to yellow to purple to brown, depending on the chile type. Although traditionally chipotle chiles are smoked dried jalapeños, Wayne likes to smoke a variety of different chiles.

Little Corn and Crescenza Tartlets

Jimtown Store, Jimtown

These tiny morsels fall under our Jimtown "first-bite" rule: As the party just gets underway and guests juggle drinks and hellos, it's important to immediately get them something attention-getting to nibble, but it should also be something that can be eaten in one swift bite. (More elaborate "two-bite" fare will come later, when everyone has settled in a bit.) These tarts also employ another of our philosophies, that of "food redundancy," or layered flavors. Here, a corn salsa tops a cornmeal pastry, for an amplification of corn, and in the mouth all the various tastes and textures are delightfully evident. Bellwether Farms' luscious Crescenza cheese makes these hors d'oeuvres completely satisfying and mouthwatering.
—Carrie Brown, owner

½ cup sweet tender corn kernels (1 large ear)
1 tablespoon finely diced red bell pepper
1 tablespoon finely chopped fresh cilantro
1 tablespoon freshly squeezed lime juice
1½ teaspoons finely chopped green onion tops

1½ teaspoons finely diced jalapeño chile
¼ teaspoon kosher salt
About 1 ounce Bellwether Farms Crescenza or other soft, mild cheese, such as Teleme
25 Cornmeal Tartlet Shells (recipe follows)

Wine-pairing suggestion: Jimtown Chardonnay, Alexander Valley

In a small bowl, combine the corn, bell pepper, cilantro, lime juice, green onion, jalapeño, and salt. Use now, or cover and refrigerate for up to 3 hours. Return to room temperature before using.

To assemble, cut the cheese into 25 pieces. Place 1 piece in each tart shell. With a small spoon, top the cheese with the corn mixture, using it all. Arrange the tarts on a serving tray and serve immediately.
Makes 25 tartlets; serves 6 to 8 as an hors d'oeuvre

Cornmeal Tartlet Shells

Jimtown Store, Jimtown

This is the perfect dough for various savory applications. It's easy to make (very forgiving in the rolling out), and the resulting little corn cups are delectably crisp, sandy textured, and buttery. It does take patience to fit the dough into the small tart plaques, but since the cups can be prepared well in advance, just make them when you have plenty of time to relax and enjoy the necessary precision of the process. You'll be rewarded by your guests' satisfaction.
—Carrie Brown, owner

1½ cups unbleached all-purpose flour
½ cup stone-ground yellow cornmeal
1 teaspoon kosher salt

¾ cup (1½ sticks) cold unsalted butter, cut into ½-inch dice
About ⅓ cup ice water

Position racks in the upper and lower thirds of the oven and preheat the oven to 375°F.

In a food processor, combine the flour, cornmeal, and salt, and pulse several times to blend. Scatter the butter over the flour mixture and pulse several times until the mixture resembles a coarse meal with bits the size of peas. Sprinkle 2 tablespoons of the water over the mixture and pulse again. Watch carefully for the dough to begin holding together. If the dough remains dry and crumbly, add more water 1 tablespoon at a time, pulsing after each addition, until the dough does begin to hold together. Do not overmix.

Turn the dough out onto a lightly floured work surface. Gather it into a ball, flatten the ball into a disk, and wrap tightly in plastic. Refrigerate for at least 30 minutes or as long as overnight for convenience.

Remove the dough from the refrigerator and let it warm slightly (10 to 15 minutes, depending on the temperature of your kitchen). On a floured work surface, gently roll the dough out to a ⅛-inch thickness.

With a 2½-inch round cookie cutter, cut the dough into rounds, transferring them as you go to a small baking sheet lined with parchment or waxed paper. Add another sheet of parchment and continue layering the rounds. Gather the scraps, reroll, and cut out the remaining rounds. You may have a few more than 25. Cover the last layer of rounds with more paper. Refrigerate for at least 30 minutes or as long as overnight. Wrap tightly in plastic if the rounds will be refrigerated for more than an hour or so.

🍃 Choose about 25 tartlet pans or mini-muffin cups 1¾ inches in diameter and about ½ inch deep. Gently fit the dough rounds, without stretching them, into the pans or cups. Prick each tart shell lightly all over with the tines of a fork. Chill the dough-lined pans and any remaining dough rounds for at least 30 minutes or as long as overnight.

🍃 Set the pans on the oven racks and bake for 10 minutes. Check the tart shells and lightly prick them again if they are puffing. Continue to bake until golden brown, another 4 to 5 minutes.

🍃 Let the tart shells cool in the pans sitting on a wire rack for 5 minutes, then carefully slip them out with your fingers and finish cooling them on the racks to room temperature.

🍃 The tart shells can be used now or they can be carefully packed between layers of parchment or waxed paper in airtight containers and held at room temperature for 1 day or frozen for up to 2 months. Thaw frozen tart shells completely at room temperature.

🍃 There is no need to reheat tart shells that have been made in advance: The pastry retains its crispness remarkably well. *Makes about twenty-five 1-inch shells*

Thai Cabbage Salad

Oakville Grocery, Healdsburg

This is one of the popular salads that we sell in our prepared-foods case. We normally carry this during the spring and summer seasons. It's easy to prepare and loaded with flavor. —Ken Hinshaw, chef

¼ head napa cabbage, cored and cut into
   1-inch pieces
¼ head green cabbage, cored and cut into
   1-inch pieces
½ bunch green onions, including green parts, sliced
2 red jalapeño or Fresno chiles, finely diced
Leaves from ⅓ bunch cilantro
½ English (hothouse) cucumber, cut in half
   lengthwise, seeded, and cut into ¼-inch slices

Dressing
3 tablespoons rice wine vinegar
1½ tablespoons sugar

¼ teaspoon minced garlic
½ teaspoon curry powder
¼ teaspoon chile oil
¼ teaspoon chile-garlic sauce (available in the Asian
   section of most supermarkets)
¼ teaspoon ground turmeric
¼ cup peanut or canola oil
½ teaspoon kosher salt
⅛ teaspoon freshly ground pepper

3 tablespoons roasted peanuts, chopped
Cilantro sprigs for garnish

🍃 In a large bowl, combine the cabbages, green onions, chiles, cilantro, and cucumber. Set aside.

🍃 Combine all the dressing ingredients in a bowl and whisk until blended. Add the dressing and all but 1 tablespoon of the chopped peanuts to the cabbage salad. Toss until well coated. Taste and adjust the seasoning.

🍃 Divide the salad among 3 to 5 salad plates. Garnish with the remaining peanuts and sprigs of cilantro. *Serves 3 to 5 as a side dish*

Wine-pairing suggestion: J Pinot Gris, J Wines

Pan-Roasted Halibut with Potato and Oxtail Hash, Summer Vegetables, and Parsley Salad

Dry Creek Kitchen, Healdsburg

Combining the freshest ingredients from the earth and the sea, this dish is the perfect meal for a late summer evening.
—Mark Purdy, chef

6 baby artichokes
1½ cups water
1½ cups dry white wine

Potato and Oxtail Hash
5 pounds oxtails
Salt and freshly ground white pepper
2 cups veal stock
1 pound small Yukon gold potatoes
1 cup (2 sticks) unsalted butter
1 onion, finely chopped
Leaves from 1 sprig thyme

8 ounces sugar snap peas, blanched for 1 minute
12 baby carrots, blanched for 1 minute
1 tablespoon unsalted butter
Salt and freshly ground pepper
6 halibut fillets (4 ounces each)
½ cup olive oil

Parsley Salad
1 shallot, thinly sliced
1 tablespoon olive oil
Leaves from 2 stems flat-leaf parsley
1 teaspoon extra virgin olive oil
Grated zest and juice of ½ lemon
Salt and freshly ground pepper

Trim artichoke leaves. Cover artichokes with 1½ cups of water and 1½ cups of wine, or enough liquid to cover. Poach for 15 to 20 minutes, or until tender. Strain the poaching liquid and reserve 1 cup. Set the artichokes aside.

For the hash, season the oxtails with salt and white pepper. Over medium heat in a large saucepan, cook 2 minutes on each side until golden brown. Place in a roasting pan and cover with veal stock. Cover pan with foil and braise for 3 hours at 200°F. Drain and reserve the braising liquid. Let the oxtails cool to the touch, then remove the meat from the bone and cartilage. Set the meat aside.

Strain the reserved oxtail braising liquid into a small saucepan and warm over medium heat. Taste and adjust the seasoning. Set aside and keep warm.

Thinly slice the potatoes and place them in a bowl of cold water. In a saucepan, melt the 1 cup butter over medium heat and sauté the onion until translucent. Drain the potatoes and add them to the pan with the reserved oxtail braising liquid and salt and pepper to taste. Cook until tender but firm, about 15 minutes, or until they are just cooked through. Gently stir

in the thyme and reserved oxtail meat and cook for 2 minutes. Transfer the hash to a bowl and keep warm.

Pour the reserved artichoke poaching liquid into a large sauté pan or skillet. Add the artichokes, snap peas, carrots, and the 1 tablespoon butter. Season with salt and pepper to taste. Cook over medium heat for about 5 minutes, or until the vegetables are heated through and the liquid is slightly reduced. Set aside and keep warm.

Season the halibut fillets with salt and pepper. In a heavy skillet over medium heat, heat the olive oil until it shimmers. Carefully place 1 fillet in the pan. Sauté until golden brown on the bottom, about 3 minutes. Repeat to cook each fillet. It is not necessary to flip the fillets, as they are fragile and thin enough to cook through on one side.

For the salad, combine all the ingredients in a small bowl and set aside.

Distribute the potato hash evenly among 6 warmed plates. Place some of the vegetables on top of the hash. Place a halibut fillet atop the vegetables. Place a portion of parsley salad atop the fish. Serve immediately.
Serves 6 as a main course

Wine-pairing suggestion: Davis Bynum Pinot Noir

Above: Roshambo Winery, opened in 2002, was designed by architects Jacques Ullman and Thomas Johnson to reflect the undulating curves of the rolling hills. The entire back wall of the visitor's center is floor-to-ceiling glass so that the tasting room of the winery seems set among the grapevines.

Preceding pages, left, top, and above: The Cabernet Sauvignon harvest in Alexander Valley starts with cutting the grapes off the vines using a small knife with a curved blade sharpened to a razor's edge. The grapes are loaded into baskets that the pickers carry to a large gondola, which is hauled when full to the winery. There, a spiral-blade conveyer moves the grapes into the mouth of a press to be crushed.

Left and above: Developing wine exudes a wonderful perfume throughout barrel rooms as the aromas escape from the porous wood of the barrels. Barrel-storing wine creates a great complexity of flavors, but the winemaker must make numerous assessments of the wine to avoid either too strong a taste of oak, which would obscure the flavors, or too little, which might deprive a wine of needed complexity. Judging how a bottled wine, which may need to age for five to ten years, will hold up with the added bouquet of oak makes the process even trickier. There are no crystal balls for winemakers, so they must use scientific training, years of experience, and instinct to make great wine. Here, wine rests in barrels in Simi Winery, *left,* and in the opulent barrel room of Ferrari-Carano Winery in Dry Creek, *above.*

Overleaf: Set at the very top of the Dry Creek Valley, Chateau Souverain looks as if it has been transplanted from the French wine country, though the shape of the tall tower seen beyond its entrance hints of a hop-kiln heritage. Designed by John Marsh Davis and built in 1974, the winery has become a popular destination because it also features beautiful gardens and a café that turns out seasonal menus that pair well with Chateau Souverain wines.

Top, above, and right: Driving through Sonoma County, the traveler runs into every sort of winery architecture. Low-profile Silver Oak Winery in Geyserville, consistently mentioned in surveys of sommeliers as the number-one requested Cabernet in America, boasts a winery building built in 1999 with an elegant courtyard entrance. The wooden building of Pezzi-King Vineyards, with wine made from organically grown grapes in the Dry Creek Valley, contrasts wildly with the French-style chateau and formal gardens of the bright mustard-colored Jordan Winery.

Overleaf, pages 210–211: Ferrari-Carano is an estate winery, raising all the grapes on its property for the wines it produces. Many wineries buy grapes from growers who choose just to raise grapes, not to make wine. Often, grape growers have long contracts with vintners when their grapes fill a particular wine-making niche or gain a reputation for excellence.

Overleaf, pages 212–213: Simi Winery's wine-tasting logo mentions "terroir," a French word that describes the subtle effects of soil, climate, temperature, and geography, as well as the local scents of grass, sea, trees, and summer breezes upon the products of a particular place. "Terroir" in Sonoma County points out the harmony between locally produced goat cheeses, a glass of Chardonnay, and freshly harvested walnuts.

YOAKIM BRIDGE
DRY CREEK VALLEY
ZINFANDEL
1998
Estate Bottled
Alc. 14.1% By Vol.

Fisher
Vineyards
1999
W
CABERNET SAUVIGNON
SONOMA COUNTY
WEDDING VINEYARD

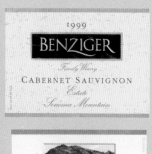

1999
BENZIGER
Family Winery
CABERNET SAUVIGNON
Estate
Sonoma Mountain

Laurel Glen
1999
SONOMA MOUNTAIN
CABERNET SAUVIGNON

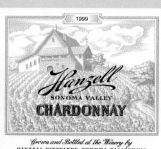

1999
Hanzell
SONOMA VALLEY
CHARDONNAY
Grown and Bottled at the Winery by
HANZELL VINEYARDS, SONOMA, CALIFORNIA
BONDED WINERY #4470 · ALCOHOL 14.5% BY VOLUME · CONTAINS SULFITES

VINTAGE 2001
ADLER FELS
RUSSIAN RIVER
SAUVIGNON BLANC

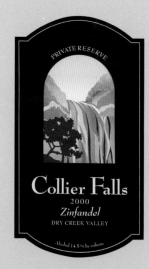

PRIVATE RESERVE
Collier Falls
2000
Zinfandel
DRY CREEK VALLEY
Alcohol 14.5% by volume

ERIC
ROSS
Occidental Vineyard
Russian River Valley

Old Vine Zinfandel
1999

Eric Ross Wines are produced from
small vineyards, hand crafted to reflect
our personal commitment to quality.

Alcohol 14.4% by Volume / 750 ML

PELLEGRINI
FAMILY VINEYARDS
CLOVERDALE
RANCH
1999
ALEXANDER VALLEY
Cabernet
Sauvignon
ALCOHOL 13% BY VOLUME
750 ML

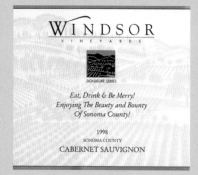

WINDSOR
VINEYARDS
SIGNATURE SERIES
Eat, Drink & Be Merry!
Enjoying The Beauty and Bounty
Of Sonoma County!
1998
SONOMA COUNTY
CABERNET SAUVIGNON

PEDRONCELLI
IN GEYSERVILLE SINCE 1927
Special Vineyard Selection
MOTHER CLONE
1999
DRY CREEK VALLEY
ZINFANDEL
SONOMA COUNTY

EST. 1974
GREBENNIKOFF
VINEYARDS
SONOMA VALLEY
MERLOT
1999
Estate Bottled
Alc. 13.4% By Vol.

1998
GROVE STREET
Alexander Valley
MERLOT

HARTFORD
COURT
LAURA'S
SONOMA COAST · CHARDONNAY
2000
HARTFORD FAMILY
WINES

WATTLE CREEK
SHIRAZ
ALEXANDER VALLEY
1999

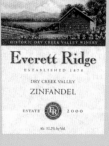

BENCHLAND WINE
MICHEL-SCHLUMBERGER
CABERNET SAUVIGNON
DRY CREEK VALLEY
1999

LEDSON
SONOMA VALLEY
MERLOT
1998

Valley of the Moon
Pinot Blanc

HISTORIC DRY CREEK VALLEY WINERY
Everett Ridge
ESTABLISHED 1878
DRY CREEK VALLEY
ZINFANDEL
ESTATE 2000
Alc. 15.2% by Vol.

PRIDE OF DRY CREEK
ESTABLISHED
ZINFANDEL

ZINFANDEL
DRY CREEK VALLEY 2000
OLD VINES / OLD CLONES

NATURALLY FERMENTED IN THIS BOTTLE
ESTABLISHED 1882
KORBEL
CALIFORNIA CHAMPAGNE
Brut
ALC. 12% BY VOL.

CHATEAU
SOUVERAIN
1999
ALEXANDER VALLEY
CABERNET SAUVIGNON

ROCHE
BARREL
RESERVE
SELECT
2000
PINOT NOIR
CARNEROS
ESTATE GROWN, PRODUCED & BOTTLED BY ROCHE WINERY SONOMA, CA · ALC. 14.9% BY VOL.

2001
ROCHIOLI
RUSSIAN RIVER VALLEY
Sauvignon Blanc
ESTATE GROWN

1999
R
A. RAFANELLI
ZINFANDEL
DRY CREEK VALLEY
SONOMA COUNTY
UNFILTERED
PRODUCED AND BOTTLED BY
A. RAFANELLI WINERY
HEALDSBURG, CALIFORNIA
Alcohol 14.2% by volume

TOPOLOS
Sonoma Valley
Zinfandel
Rossi Ranch
1999
UNFINED

PRODUCED & BOTTLED BY TOPOLOS
AT RUSSIAN RIVER VINEYARDS, FORESTVILLE, CA. USA
WITH ORGANICALLY GROWN GRAPES
ALCOHOL 14.5% BY VOLUME. CONTAINS SULFITES

2000

QUIVIRA
DRY CREEK VALLEY

ZINFANDEL
Dry Creek Valley

Venus

VINEYARDS

SELENE
2000 ALEXANDER VALLEY
SEMILLON
ALC. 13.5% BY VOL.

2001
NALLE
SONOMA COUNTY
DRY CREEK VALLEY
ZINFANDEL
ALC. 13.5% BY VOL.
PRODUCED AND BOTTLED BY NALLE WINERY
HEALDSBURG, CALIFORNIA

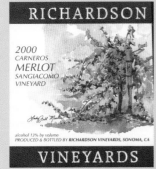

RICHARDSON
2000
CARNEROS
MERLOT
SANGIACOMO
VINEYARD

alcohol 13% by volume
PRODUCED & BOTTLED BY RICHARDSON VINEYARDS, SONOMA, CA

VINEYARDS

Amphora
UNFILTERED
2000
ALC. 13.5% BY VOLUME

Zinfandel
Dry Creek Valley
La Loma Block / Mounts Vineyard

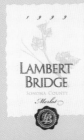

1 9 9 9

LAMBERT
BRIDGE
SONOMA COUNTY
Merlot

Kistler
Occidental Vineyard
Cuvée Elizabeth

Sonoma Coast Pinot Noir   2000
ALC 14.1% BY VOL.

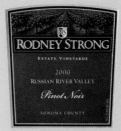

RODNEY STRONG
ESTATE VINEYARDS
2000
RUSSIAN RIVER VALLEY
Pinot Noir
SONOMA COUNTY

1997 Dry Creek Valley
Syrah
Cherry blossoms, violet leaves
red dust, old citrus trees.
The stone rests against a vine's trunk;
a long roll down, dust.

PRODUCED & BOTTLED BY FRICK WINERY. B.W. 4771
23072 WALLING RD., GEYSERVILLE, CALIFORNIA USA
Alcohol by Volume 13.6%

RAVENS
WOOD
1 9 9 9
NAPA VALLEY
ZINFANDEL
ALCOHOL 14.9% BY VOL.

MacMurray
RANCH
RUSSIAN RIVER VALLEY
PINOT NOIR

2000

1999 SONOMA COUNTY
ZINFANDEL

Marietta

PRODUCED AND BOTTLED BY
MARIETTA
CELLARS
GEYSERVILLE
CALIFORNIA
ALCOHOL 14.5% BY VOL.

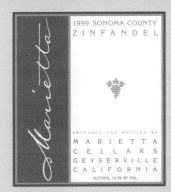

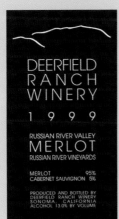

DEERFIELD
RANCH
WINERY
1 9 9 9
RUSSIAN RIVER VALLEY
MERLOT
RUSSIAN RIVER VINEYARDS
MERLOT   95%
CABERNET SAUVIGNON 5%
PRODUCED AND BOTTLED BY
DEERFIELD RANCH WINERY
SONOMA, CALIFORNIA
ALCOHOL 13.0% BY VOLUME

GOLDEN CREEK
SONOMA COUNTY
· SHIRAZ ·
1999
RESERVE
LADI'S VINEYARD · ESTATE GROWN

BLACKSTONE
WINERY
Cabernet Sauvignon
CALIFORNIA
1 9 9 9
ALC. 13.5% VOL.

COTURRI
2000
Merlot
Mische Vineyard
Sonoma Valley
PRODUCED AND BOTTLED BY
H. Coturri & Sons, Ltd.
GLEN ELLEN, CA

DENATALE
FAMILY
ESTATE
COMBINES
THE STRONG
TRADITION OF
FAMILY WINE
MAKING WITH
A SPECIAL
HANDS-ON
VINE TO WINE
APPROACH
ON THEIR
UNIQUE
ESTATE.

DeNatale
ESTATE
2000
RUSSIAN RIVER VALLEY
Pinot Noir
125 CASES PRODUCED
ALC. 13.5% BY VOLUME

GROWN,
PRODUCED
AND BOTTLED
BY DENATALE
FAMILY ESTATE
HEALDSBURG,
SONOMA
COUNTY,
CALIFORNIA
CONTAINS SULFITES

GOVERNMENT
WARNING: ...

PETERSON
1999
DRY CREEK VALLEY
ZINFANDEL
SONOMA COUNTY

ALBINI
FAMILY VINEYARDS
RUSSIAN RIVER VALLEY
19 ZINFANDEL 99
DRY FARMED
ALC. 14.2%   BW 5634

HOMEWOOD
WINERY
BARBERA
2001
Sonoma Valley
Kunde Vineyard
PRODUCED & BOTTLED BY HOMEWOOD WINERY
SONOMA, CA · 12½% ALC. BY VOL. CONTAINS SULFITES

Tarius
1999
Pinot Noir
RUSSIAN RIVER VALLEY
ALC. BY VOL. 14.1%

GLORIA FERRER

FERMENTED IN THIS BOTTLE

PRODUCED AND BOTTLED
BY FREIXENET SONOMA CAVES
SONOMA, CALIFORNIA USA

SONOMA COUNTY MÉTHODE CHAMPENOISE

ALCOHOL 12%
BY VOLUME
750 ML

BLANC
DE NOIRS

ESTATE BOTTLED
IRON HORSE
Classic Vintage Brut
SPARKLING WINE·SONOMA COUNTY·GREEN VALLEY
ALC. 13.5% BY VOL.   1997   NET VOL. 750 ML.

GLENLYON
NE OBLIVISCARIS
VINEYARDS
& WINERY

PARADISE
RIDGE
SAUVIGNON BLANC
GRANDVIEW VINEYARD
SONOMA COUNTY
2001

2000
ESTATE ZINFANDEL
DRY CREEK VALLEY
Talty
WILLIAM TALTY VINEYARDS

McCRAY RIDGE

1999
Merlot
TWO MOON VINEYARD
DRY CREEK VALLEY

ALC. 14.1% BY VOL.

ARROWOOD
1999
RUSSIAN RIVER VALLEY
Syrah
SARALEE'S VINEYARD

2000

Armida
Zinfandel
Maple Vineyard
Dry Creek Valley
alc. 15.0% by vol.

ISLAND BLOCK
ESTATE CHARDONNAY
ALEXANDER VALLEY

2000

MURPHY-GOODE

LANDMARK
DAMARIS
2000

WILLIAMS
SELYEM

1999
PINOT NOIR
Russian River Valley
ROCHIOLI RIVERBLOCK VINEYARD
Alcohol by Volume 14.5 Percent

Produced & Bottled by
Williams & Selyem Winery
6575 Westside Rd., Healdsburg, Ca 95448

WELLINGTON
VINEYARDS

2000
SONOMA COUNTY
SYRAH

B.R. COHN

1999 SONOMA VALLEY
CABERNET SAUVIGNON
Olive Hill Estate Vineyards

CANYON
ROAD
2000
CABERNET
SAUVIGNON
california

SONOMA COUNTY
1998

HANS FAHDEN

MOUNTAIN CUVÉE
CABERNET SAUVIGNON
ALC 13.5% BY VOL.

HANNA

1999
Cabernet Sauvignon
ALEXANDER VALLEY
Proprietor Grown

ALCOHOL
BY
VOLUME
14.5%

KEEGAN

2000
PINOT NOIR
RUSSIAN RIVER VALLEY

E BLOCK

LANCASTER
Estate

1999

ESTATE BOTTLED

RED WINE

ALEXANDER VALLEY

PROPRIETOR

ALC. 14.2% BY VOL.

PK
PEZZI
KING

1999
VINTAGE
Zinfandel
ESTATE BOTTLED

1999
Mill Creek
VINEYARDS & WINERY
DRY CREEK VALLEY
MERLOT
Estate Bottled

CASTLE

1999
LOS CARNEROS
Pinot Noir

1997 RESERVE

CHARDONNAY
SONOMA VALLEY 60% • NAPA VALLEY 40%

IMAGERY
Artist Collection

KAZ 1998
Vineyard & Winery

Slide
Chardonnay
Sonoma Valley   Alc.13.2% by Vol.

CHATEAU ST JEAN

2000
CHARDONNAY
SONOMA COUNTY

VÉRITÉ
La Joie
1999
SONOMA COUNTY RED WINE

1999
DEHLINGER
Pinot Noir
• Octagon •
RUSSIAN RIVER VALLEY
ESTATE BOTTLED

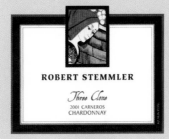

ROBERT STEMMLER
Three Clone
2001 CARNEROS
CHARDONNAY

Smothers Winery
REMICK RIDGE
VINEYARDS
Cabernet Sauvignon
SONOMA VALLEY
1996
ALCOHOL 14.30% BY VOLUME
LIMITED 125 CASES PRODUCED

LIMERICK LANE
1999
Zinfandel
COLLINS VINEYARD
ESTATE BOTTLED • UNFILTERED
RUSSIAN RIVER VALLEY
ALC 14.6% BY VOL

DUTTON
Goldfield
2000
Dutton Ranch
RUSSIAN RIVER VALLEY
Pinot Noir

2000
Buena Vista
SAUVIGNON BLANC
CALIFORNIA

Annapolis Winery

Los Chamizal Vineyard

HAYWOOD
ESTATE
1999
LOS CHAMIZAL VINEYARD
ZINFANDEL
SONOMA VALLEY

STRYKER
ZINFANDEL
OLD VINE ESTATE
ALEXANDER VALLEY
2000

MERRY EDWARDS
1999
RUSSIAN RIVER VALLEY
PINOT NOIR
ALCOHOL 14.2% BY VOLUME

SAUSAL
1997
ALEXANDER VALLEY
SANGIOVESE

ESTATE BOTTLED
GUNDLACH BUNDSCHU
Cabernet Sauvignon
1999
RHINEFARM VINEYARD
SONOMA VALLEY
GROWN, PRODUCED & BOTTLED ON RHINEFARM VINEYARD
ESTABLISHED IN 1858

DOMAINE•SAINT•GEORGE
ST
GEORGE
1905
Cabernet Sauvignon
CALIFORNIA

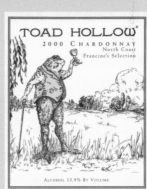

TOAD HOLLOW®
2000 CHARDONNAY
North Coast
Francine's Selection
ALCOHOL 13.9% By Volume

1999
RUSSIAN
RIVER
VALLEY
PINOT NOIR
ESTATE BOTTLED
J

FAVERO
1999
Sonoma Valley
MONTE DI SASSI
Sangiovese 65% - Cabernet 35%
ALCOHOL 13.4% BY VOLUME

1999
ESTATE BOTTLED
Alexander Valley Vineyards
CABERNET SAUVIGNON
ALEXANDER VALLEY
ALCOHOL 13.8 PERCENT BY VOLUME
WETZEL FAMILY ESTATE

1998
BELVEDERE
SONOMA COUNTY
HEALDSBURG RANCHES
CABERNET SAUVIGNON

DE LOACH
2000
ESTATE BOTTLED
ZINFANDEL
RUSSIAN RIVER VALLEY

Walker Station
Chardonnay
RUSSIAN RIVER VALLEY
2000

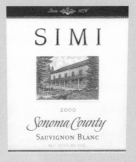

Since 1876
SIMI
2000
Sonoma County
SAUVIGNON BLANC

PRODUCED & BOTTLED BY MacROSTIE WINERY
SONOMA, CA USA • WHITE TABLE WINE
2000
MACROSTIE
CHARDONNAY
CARNEROS

ESTATE BOTTLED
1997
Johnson's
ALEXANDER
VALLEY WINES
Alexander Valley
Chardonnay

BROGAN
CELLARS
PINOT NOIR
2001
RUSSIAN RIVER VALLEY
alcohol 13.5% by volume
PRODUCED & BOTTLED BY
BROGAN CELLARS
3232B DRY CREEK ROAD
HEALDSBURG, CA 95448

MAZZOCCO
1999
SONOMA COUNTY
CHARDONNAY
Winemaker's Select

2000
FOPPIANO
VINEYARDS
ESTABLISHED 1896
PETITE SIRAH
SONOMA COUNTY

TARA BELLA
WINERY & VINEYARDS

1997
Russian River Valley
Trenton Estate Vineyard
Pentagon   Pinot Noir   Reserve
Joseph Swan Vineyards
Grown, Produced and Bottled by Joseph Swan Vineyards
Forestville, California. Alcohol 13.5% by Volume

STONESTREET
1999
CHARDONNAY
Sonoma County
ALCOHOL 13.5% BY VOLUME

KENDALL-JACKSON
CHARDONNAY
California
2000
VINTNER'S RESERVE*

ST·FRANCIS
SONOMA COUNTY
CABERNET SAUVIGNON

RUSSIAN HILL
1999 PINOT NOIR
RUSSIAN RIVER VALLEY

TAFT
STREET
2001
RUSSIAN RIVER VALLEY
Sauvignon
Blanc
ALC. 13.6% BY VOL.

Pastori Wines
ESTATE   1997
BOTTLED
NORTHERN SONOMA
PREMIUM
ZINFANDEL
ALCOHOL 15% BY VOLUME
PRODUCED AND BOTTLED BY
Pastori Winery   CONTAINS SULFITES
CLOVERDALE, SONOMA COUNTY, CALIFORNIA

SCHUG
1999
CARNEROS
PINOT NOIR
barrel aged 16 months
HERITAGE   RESERVE
ALC. 13.5% VOL.

Field Stone
1998
Staten Family Reserve
CABERNET SAUVIGNON
Alexander Valley
Estate Bottled
GROWN, PRODUCED & BOTTLED
BY FIELD STONE WINERY
HEALDSBURG, CALIFORNIA, USA
ALCOHOL 14.1% BY VOLUME

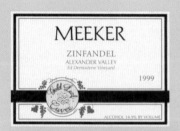
MEEKER
ZINFANDEL
ALEXANDER VALLEY
Ed Demostene Vineyard
1999
Gold Leaf Cuvée
ALCOHOL 14.9% BY VOLUME

HUNTINGTON
2000 ALEXANDER VALLEY
MERLOT
ALC. 13.5% By Vol.

RESERVE
GEYSER PEAK
1998 Sonoma County Cabernet Sauvignon

Raymond Burr
CABERNET SAUVIGNON
Dry Creek Valley
1998
ALC. 14.4% BY VOL.

ROBERT HUNTER
Extended
Tirage
1996
BRUT DE NOIRS
SONOMA VALLEY SPARKLING WINE
750 ML / ALCOHOL 12% BY VOL
PRODUCED AND BOTTLED BY ROBERT HUNTER WINERY BWCA 5320, SONOMA, CA USA

VINTAGE 2000
SANGIOVESE
Our family first planted Italian
varietals in 1910 near Chianti Station in
Sonoma County. The steam locomotive
was vital in delivering our grandparents'
grapes and wines to market.
ALEXANDER VALLEY
SINCE 1895
SEGHESIO
Family Vineyards
ALC. 14.8%   CONTENTS
BY VOL.   750ML

SIDURI
HIRSCH VINEYARD
SONOMA COAST PINOT NOIR
2000
ALC. 14.1% BY VOL.

SEBASTIANI
FAMILY OWNED SINCE 1904
COHEN VINEYARD
2000
RUSSIAN RIVER VALLEY
SAUVIGNON BLANC

RIDGE   2000
CALIFORNIA
LYTTON SPRINGS
ESTATE GROWN: 80% ZINFANDEL, 20% PETITE SIRAH
DRY CREEK VALLEY   ALCOHOL 14.8% BY VOLUME
PRODUCED AND BOTTLED BY RIDGE VINEYARDS, INC.   BW 4488
17100 MONTE BELLO ROAD, BOX 1810, CUPERTINO, CALIFORNIA 95015

RESERVE
CHATEAU DIANA
CALIFORNIA
CHARDONNAY
WINE PRODUCT

Dry Creek Vineyard.
SONOMA COUNTY
2001 FUMÉ BLANC
DRY SAUVIGNON BLANC

1998
WALTER HANSEL
Hansel Family Vineyards
RUSSIAN RIVER VALLEY
Cuvée Alyce
Chardonnay

KENWOOD
2000
SONOMA COUNTY
SAUVIGNON BLANC
ALCOHOL 13.8% BY VOLUME

MIETZ
SONOMA COUNTY 2000
SanGiovese

MARK WEST
20 01
Etna Valley Pinot Noir
ALC. 13.9% BY VOL.

1999
PETER MICHAEL
WINERY
'Les Pavots'
68% CABERNET SAUVIGNON, 17% MERLOT, 15% CABERNET FRANC
FROM KNIGHTS VALLEY • ALCOHOL 14.1% BY VOLUME
ESTATE BOTTLED BY PETER MICHAEL • CALISTOGA, CALIFORNIA

1999
PINOT NOIR
CARNEROS
ALC. BY VOL 14.1%
DOMAINE DANICA

CLOS DU BOIS
1998
ALEXANDER VALLEY RESERVE
Cabernet Sauvignon
ALEXANDER VALLEY
ALC. 14.1% BY VOL.

2000
FERRARI·CARANO
ALEXANDER VALLEY
Chardonnay
ALCOHOL 13.7% BY VOLUME

SELBY
2000
SONOMA COUNTY
ZINFANDEL
OLD VINES
ALC. 15.5% BY VOL.

RANCHO
ZABACO
SONOMA HERITAGE VINES
2000
ZINFANDEL
SONOMA COUNTY

Teldeschi
1996
PETITE SIRAH
DRY CREEK VALLEY
CELLARED & BOTTLED BY TELDESCHI
WINE CELLARS, HEALDSBURG, CA.
ALCOHOL 14.2% BY VOLUME

Jordan
2000
CHARDONNAY
RUSSIAN RIVER VALLEY

Chandelle
The Spirit of Flight
The Pan American China Clipper
Martin M-130
by Frank Loudin
CHANDELLE OF SONOMA
Box 2167, Glen Ellen CA 95442 • 800-544-8890

WhiteOak
1999
ESTATE BOTTLED
Zinfandel
ALEXANDER VALLEY
ALC. 14.9% BY VOL.

1998
Stuhlmuller Vineyards
CABERNET SAUVIGNON
Alexander Valley • Sonoma County

ESTATE BOTTLED
PORTER CREEK
1999
RUSSIAN RIVER VALLEY
PINOT NOIR
CREEKSIDE VINEYARD
ALCOHOL 13.5% BY VOLUME

SILVER OAK
1997
Alexander Valley Cabernet Sauvignon

LA CREMA
2000 PINOT NOIR
RUSSIAN RIVER VALLEY

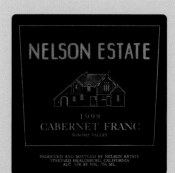
2000
ABUNDANCE VINEYARDS
MENCARINI VINEYARDS
OLD VINE ZINFANDEL
LODI
Robert Goyette

Est. 1890
FREI BROTHERS
RESERVE
vintage 2000
Alexander Valley
CABERNET SAUVIGNON
NORTHERN SONOMA

SABLE RIDGE
VINEYARDS
PETITE SIRAH
RUSSIAN RIVER
VALLEY
2000

RVTZ
CELLARS
RUSSIAN RIVER VALLEY
Sales & Administrative Office:
1438 3rd Street, San Rafael, CA 94901
Phone: (415) 482-6563 Fax: (415) 482-6391
Winery & Cave:
3637 Frei Road, Sebastopol, CA 95473
Phone: (707) 823-6373 Fax: (707) 823-4364

BRADFORD
MOUNTAIN
Grist Vineyard
ZINFANDEL
DRY CREEK VALLEY
2000
ALCOHOL 14.9 PERCENT BY VOLUME

NELSON ESTATE
1998
CABERNET FRANC
SONOMA VALLEY
PRODUCED AND BOTTLED BY NELSON ESTATE
VINEYARD HEALDSBURG, CALIFORNIA
ALC. 13% BY VOL. 750 ML.

ESTATE BOTTLED
KUNDE
2000 CHARDONNAY
SONOMA VALLEY

UNTI
DRY CREEK VALLEY
SYRAH
2000
GROWN, PRODUCED AND BOTTLED BY UNTI VINEYARDS
HEALDSBURG CALIFORNIA ALCOHOL 14.5% BY VOLUME

CLINE
2000
Syrah
Sonoma County
ALCOHOL 13.5% BY VOLUME

SPECIAL SELECTION
STONE CREEK
Cabernet Sauvignon
2000 CALIFORNIA

FORCHINI
VINEYARDS & WINERY

SACCHI, CARAVAGGIO, UFFIZI GALLERY, FLORENCE

ZINFANDEL
Papa Nonne
Old Vine Clone Dry Creek Valley
1999 Estate Bottled

PRODUCED & BOTTLED BY FORCHINI VINEYARDS & WINERY
HEALDSBURG, SONOMA COUNTY, CA
ALC. 13.9 % BY VOL. 750 ML

BAREFOOT

CALIFORNIA
CHARDONNAY
ALC. 13.0% BY VOL

ESTATE BOTTLED
1998
MOSAIC
*Just as distinct elements of
color come together to create art,*
ALEXANDER VALLEY
MERITAGE
our intricately blended red
67% CABERNET SAUVIGNON · 21% MERLOT
varietals combine to form a
8% MALBEC · 4% CABERNET FRANC
complex mosaic of wine.

Battaglini
Estate · Winery
Twin Pines Ranch

Russian River Valley
2000 Zinfandel
Unfined   Alcohol 15.0% Vol.   Old Vines

1998

OPTIMA

ALEXANDER
VALLEY
CABERNET
SAUVIGNON

DuNah

CHARDONNAY
2001
DeDee's Vineyard
SONOMA COAST
RESERVE

ESTATE GROWN   2000   ESTATE BOTTLED

MARIMAR
TORRES ESTATE

DON MIGUEL VINEYARD
CHARDONNAY
RUSSIAN RIVER VALLEY

32
ALEXANDER VALLEY

TRENTADUE

2000
ALEXANDER VALLEY

Petite Sirah

ESTATE BOTTLED
ALC. 14.4% BY VOL.

ACORN

2000
HERITAGE VINES
ZINFANDEL
ALEGRÍA VINEYARDS
RUSSIAN RIVER VALLEY

SONOMA
CREEK

SONOMA CREEK
2000 Sonoma County
MERLOT
ALC. 13.5% BY VOL.

sapphire

hill

RUSSIAN RIVER VALLEY
2000
CHARDONNAY

HOP KILN

1999
RUSSIAN RIVER VALLEY
ZINFANDEL
OLD WINDMILL VINEYARD

ALCOHOL 15.4% BY VOLUME

Lake
SONOMA

WINERY IN
THE DRY CREEK
VALLEY

1999
DRY CREEK VALLEY
ZINFANDEL
Heck Family Cellars Selection

ALC. 14.9% BY VOL

Rabbit Ridge

1999
SONOMA COUNTY
ZINFANDEL
ALC. 13.9% BY VOL.

Dutch Bill Creek

2000
Chardonnay
Russian River Valley

HEINTZ RANCH
Occidental
ALCOHOL 14.2% BY VOL.

DAVIS
BYNUM

2000
roshambo
sauvignon
blanc

2000
RUSSIAN RIVER VALLEY
LINDLEYS' KNOLL
ESTATE BOTTLED PINOT NOIR
ALC. 13.8% BY VOL.

2000
RUSSIAN RIVER VALLEY

LYNMAR
Quail Hill Vineyard
1999 QUAIL CUVÉE
Russian River Valley
PINOT NOIR
ALCOHOL 14.7% BY VOLUME

ALDER
BROOK

2000
ZINFANDEL OVOC
DRY CREEK VALLEY

David
Coffaro

2001
ESTATE CUVÉE
Dry Creek Valley Red Wine
Estate Bottled · Unfiltered/Unfined

FRITZ WINERY

DUTTON
RANCH
RUSSIAN RIVER VALLEY

2000

CHARDONNAY

RRV
RIVER ROAD
VINEYARDS
2000
RUSSIAN RIVER VALLEY
CHARDONNAY
ALCOHOL 13.0% BY VOLUME

MATANZAS
CREEK
WINERY
1999 Chardonnay
Sonoma Valley

GARY FARRELL
2000
Sonoma County
Pinot Noir

Russian River Valley

CHRISTOPHER CREEK

2000
Petite Sirah
ESTATE BOTTLED
Russian River Valley

Alcohol 13.5% by Volume

2000
LAURIER.
MERLOT
DRY CREEK VALLEY
ALC. 12.5% BY VOL.

MOONDANCE
CELLARS
1999 ZINFANDEL
Napa Valley

Gallo Family's
GALLO of **SONOMA**
ALEXANDER VALLEY
Sangiovese

BARREL AGED   1999

CALIFORNIA HISTORY, ITALIAN TRADITION
MARTINI & PRATI

2000 SONOMA COUNTY
RED WINE
TESORO di ELMO

VINTAGE 1999

The Cutrer

APPELLATION RUSSIAN RIVER VALLEY

ESTATE BOTTLED
SONOMA-CUTRER

RUSSIAN RIVER VALLEY CHARDONNAY BOTTLED BY SONOMA-CUTRER, WINDSOR, CA. ALC. 14.2% BY VOL.

MOON MOUNTAIN
VINEYARD

2000
CABERNET
SAUVIGNON
Estate
SONOMA VALLEY

Hog
Wilde

Cabernet
Sauvignon
1999

Fanucchi
VINEYARDS

1999
**OLD VINE
ZINFANDEL**

The Fanucchi Wood Road Vineyard™
in The Russian River Valley
of Sonoma County

Growing in Harmony With Nature Since 1906!
Alcohol 14.1% by Vol.

GAN EDEN

1997
CABERNET SAUVIGNON
Limited Reserve
ALC. 13% BY VOL.

BANNISTER

1999 RUSSIAN RIVER VALLEY CHARDONNAY
ROCHIOLI AND ALLEN VINEYARDS

ESTATE BOTTLED
HILLSIDE SELECT · UNFILTERED

MAYO
FAMILY WINERY
2000
SONOMA VALLEY
LAUREL HILL VINEYARD
Chardonnay
ALC. 13.9 BY VOL.

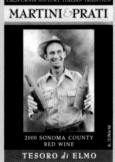

ACKNOWLEDGMENTS

This book could never have been completed without the help of the growers, farmers, wine makers, and restaurateurs of Sonoma County. Their generosity with both time and information was staggering. Special thanks go to those who allowed us access to their homes, restaurants, kitchens, or places of business in order to take many of the photographs for the book. The following proprietors and chefs graciously shared both their time and their resources with us over the last year to this end: The Weber family, Della Fattoria Bakery, The Callahan family, Bellwether Farms, Laura Chenel, Chester Aaron, Jim Reichardt, Sonoma Poultry Company, Hector Alvarez, Hector's Bees, Michael Watchorn, Hog Island Oyster Company, Stan DeVoto, DeVoto Gardens, Colleen McGlynn and Ridgely Evers, DaVero Olive Oil, The Kozlowski family, Kozlowski Farms, Lee and Wayne James, Tierra Vegetables, Carrie Brown, Jimtown Store, Todd Muir, St. Francis Winery Kitchen, Duskie Estes and John Stewart, Zazu, Sondra Berstein and John Toulouze, The Girl & The Fig, Joe Vitale, The General's Daughter, Dan and Kathleen Berman, MIXX, and Mark Purdy, Dry Creek Kitchen.

Special thanks are due as well to chef John Ash for not only contributing the foreword to the book, but also for inspiring us and so many other Sonoma County natives and visitors over the years through his love of Sonoma's bounty.

Our book would not have been published without the nurturing support of our publisher Ten Speed Press. We would like to thank publisher Kirsty Melville, owner Phil Wood, editor Annie Nelson, production manager Hal Hershey, and the staff at Ten Speed who so enthusiastically helped bring the book to market.

Many people helped us on a daily basis to produce the book: Kristen Wurz, design production; Blake Hallanan, project management; Annie Fogarty for keeping Robert Holmes Photography running so smoothly during Bob's long absences; Melissa Sweet, illustrator and cartographer; and Carolyn Miller, Linda Bouchard, Thom Elkjer, and Ken Dellapenta for editorial services.

To our families Bobbie, Emma and Hannah Holmes, Tom and Aidan Johnson, and Daniel and Arann Harris, we are most grateful for their companionship and unconditional support.

We cannot help but acknowledge and thank Michele Anna Jordan, whose earlier book first highlighted the magnificence of Sonoma County food and wine, and whose weekly newspaper columns focus on local farmers and farmers' markets. Our thanks as well to Edmond Hakin and Kouros Tavakoli of Photo Sprint in Mill Valley for handling the processing of huge quantities of film so efficiently; George Olson of *Sunset* magazine for not only giving the photographer so many opportunities to explore Sonoma County, but also for his friendship and advice; Barbara Bowman of Boss Dog Marketing and Marie Gewirtz of Marie Gewirtz Public Relations, both long involved in the Sonoma County Chefs Tasting, which brought together Sonoma County chefs, vintners, and farmers for a gala celebration of Sonoma County products. Their insight into Sonoma County food and wine producers helped immensely during the formation of the book. A grateful thanks as well to Gaye LeBaron, the pre-eminent historian of Sonoma County, whose books and columns help us all remember or learn the history of Sonoma County's agricultural past. And finally, thanks go to our friend photographer Charles O'Rear, whose beautiful book on Napa Valley inspired us to explore the county closer to our hearts. His book became the benchmark for all our efforts.

—Jennifer Barry, Robert Holmes, and Mimi Luebbermann

Sonoma County

Rockpile
Sonoma County
Sonoma County

CLOVERDALE

GEYSERVILLE

Alexander Valley

LAKE SONOMA

Dry Creek Valley

Knights Valley

HEALDSBURG

Russian River

128

Sonoma Coast

FORT ROSS

1

Northern Sonoma

Chalk Hill

101

Coastal Range

GUERNEVILLE

116

Russian River Valley

SANTA ROSA

Sonoma County

Mayacamas Mts.

Jenner

FORESTVILLE

12

Pacific Ocean

116

12

Sonoma Valley

Green Valley

GLEN ELLEN

OCCIDENTAL   SEBASTOPOL

12

116

BODEGA

Sonoma Mts.

Sonoma Mountain

SONOMA

Bodega Bay

1

101

PETALUMA

12 121 12

116

Tomales Bay

116

121

Carneros

Sonoma Valley

37

LIST OF WINERIES

1. A. Rafanelli 4C
2. Abundance 8F
3. Acorn 5C
4. Adler Fels 7E
5. Albini 5C
6. Alderbrook 5C
7. Alexander Valley 5C
8. Amphora 4C
9. Annapolis 1B
10. Armida 5C
11. Arrowood 8F
12. B.R. Cohn 8F
13. Bannister 5C
14. Barefoot Cellars 6D
15. Bartholomew Park 9G
16. Battaglini 6D
17. Bellerose 4C
18. Belvedere 5D
19. Benziger 8F
20. Blackstone 8E
21. Bradford Mountain 5C
22. Braren Pauli 6G
23. Brogan Cellars 4B
24. Buena Vista 9G
25. Canyon Road 5B
26. Castle 8F
27. Chalk Hill 6D
28. Chandelle 8F
29. Chateau Diana 4B
30. Chateau Souverain 5B
31. Chateau St. Jean 8E
32. Christopher Creek 5C
33. Cline Cellars 8H
34. Clos Du Bois 5B
35. Collier Falls 4B

36. Coturri 7F
37. Crane Canyon 7E
38. David Caffaro 4B
39. Davis Bynum 5D
40. De Loach 5E
41. de Lorimier 5B
42. Deerfield Ranch 7E
43. Dehlinger 5E
44. DeNatale 5D
45. Domaine Danica 6D
46. Domaine St. George 5C
47. Dry Creek 4B
48. DuNah Vineyard 5E
49. Dutch Bill Creek 4E
50. Dutton-Goldfield 5E
51. E. & J. Gallo 4B
52. Eric Ross 4E
53. Everett Ridge 5C
54. F. Teldeschi 4B
55. Fanucchi Vineyards 5E
56. Favero 8G
57. Ferrari-Carano 4B
58. Field Stone 5C
59. Fisher 7D
60. Foppiano 5C
61. Forchini 4B
62. Frei Brothers 5D
63. Frick 4B
64. Fritz 4A
65. Gan Eden 5E
66. Gary Farrell 5D
67. Geyser Peak 4B
68. Glen Ellen 8F
69. GlenLyon 8F
70. Gloria Ferrer 8H

71. Golden Creek 6D
72. Grebennikoff Vineyards 9G
73. Grove Street 4C
74. Gundlach-Bundschu 9G
75. Hafner 5B
76. Hanna 5C
77. Hans Fahden 7D
78. Hanzell 8F
79. Hartford Court 4D
80. Haywood 8G
81. Homewood 9G
82. Hop Kiln 5D
83. Huntington 6D
84. Imagery Estate 8F
85. Iron Horse 4E
86. J Wines 5D
87. J. Pedroncelli 4B
88. J. Rochioli 5D
89. Johnson's 5C
90. Jordan 5C
91. Joseph Swan 5E
92. Kaz 7E
93. Keegan Cellars 5D
94. Kendall-Jackson 5C
95. Kenwood 8E
96. Kistler 5E
97. Korbel 4D
98. Kunde Estate 8E
99. La Crema 5D
100. Lake Sonoma 4B
101. Lambert Bridge 4C
102. Lancaster Estate 5C
103. Landmark 7E
104. Laurel Glen 7F
105. Laurier 8G

106. Ledson 7E
107. Limerick Lane 5C
108. Lynmar 5E
109. MacMurray Ranch 5D
110. MacRostie 8G
111. Marietta 4B
112. Marimar Torres 4E
113. Mark West 5E
114. Martinelli 5E
115. Martini & Prati 5E
116. Matanzas Creek 7F
117. Mayo 7E
118. Mazzocco 4C
119. McCray Ridge 4C
120. Meeker 4B
121. Merry Edwards 4D
122. Michel-Schlumberger 4C
123. Mietz 5C
124. Mill Creek 5C
125. Moon Mountain 8F
126. Moondance Cellars 8E
127. Murphy-Goode 5B
128. Nalle 4B
129. Nelson Estate 8E
130. Optima 5C
131. Paradise Ridge 6E
132. Pastori 4B
133. Pellegrini Family 6E
134. Peter Michael 7C
135. Peterson 4C
136. Pezzi-King 4C
137. Philip Staley 4C
138. Porter Creek 4D
139. Preston 4B
140. Pride Mountain 7D

141. Quivira 4B
142. Rabbit Ridge 5D
143. Rancho Zabaco 4C
144. Ravenswood 8F
145. Raymond Burr 4B
146. Richardson 9G
147. Ridge/Lytton Springs 4C
148. River Road 5E
149. Robert Hunter 8H
150. Robert Stemmler 8G
151. Roche 8H
152. Rodney Strong 5C
153. Roshambo 5D
154. Russian Hill 5C
155. Rutz 5E
156. Sable Ridge 7E
157. Sapphire Hill 5C
158. Sausal 5C
159. Schug 8G
160. Sebastiani 8G
161. Sebastopol 4E
162. Seghesio 4C
163. Selby 5C
164. Seven Lions 5E
165. Siduri 6E
166. Silver Oak 4B
167. Simi 5C
168. Smothers/Remick Ridge 8E
169. Sonoma Creek 8H
170. Sonoma Cutrer 5E
171. St. Francis 8E
172. Stone Creek 8E
173. Stonestreet 5C
174. Stryker 5C
175. Stuhlmuller 5C

176. Sunce Winery 6E
177. Taft Street 5E
178. Tantalus 8H
179. Tara Bella 6D
180. Tarius 5E
181. Toad Hollow 5D
182. Topolos 4E
183. Trentadue 5B
184. Unti 4C
185. Valley of the Moon 8F
186. Venus 5D
187. Vérité 5C
188. Viansa 8H
189. Walker Station 3E
190. Walter Hansel 5D
191. Wattle Creek 3A
192. Wellington 7F
193. White Oak 5C
194. Wild Hog 2D
195. William Talty 4B
196. Williams Selyem 5D
197. Windsor 5C
198. Yoakim Bridge 4B

Appellations are shown in italics

RESOURCES & CONTRIBUTORS

BAKERIES

Artisan Bakers, p. 57
750 West Napa St.
Sonoma 95476
(707) 939-1765

Della Fattoria, p. 56
1159 Skillman Ln.
Petaluma 94952
(707) 762-1722

Downtown Bakery &
Creamery, p. 118
308A Center St.
Healdsburg 95448
(707) 431-2719

DAIRY/CHEESE

Bellwether Farms, pp. 86, 194
P.O. Box 299
Valley Ford 94972
(707) 763-0993
bellwethercheese.com

Bodega Goat Cheese, p. 40
P.O. Box 223
Bodega 94922
(707) 876-3483

Clover-Stornetta Farms
91 Lakeville Rd.
Petaluma 94952
(707) 778-8448

Laura Chenel Chevre, pp. 41, 42
315 Second St.
East Sonoma 95476
(707) 996-4477

Redwood Hill Farm, p. 185
10855 Occidental Rd.
Sebastopol 95472
(707) 823-8250

Sonoma Cheese Factory
2 West Spain St.
Sonoma 95476
(707) 996-1931
sonomajack.com

Spring Hill Cheese
4235 Spring Hill Rd.
Petaluma 94952
(707) 762-3446

Vella Cheese Co., p. 78
315 Second St. East
Sonoma 95476
(800) 848-0505

FARMS (ANIMALS)

C.K. Lamb, p. 184
11100 Los Amigos Rd.
Healdsburg 95448
(707) 431-8161

Petaluma Farms
700 Cavanaugh Lane
Petaluma 94952
(707) 763-0921

Petaluma Poultry
2700 Lakeville Hwy.
Petaluma 94952
(707) 763-1904

Sonoma Poultry Company
(Liberty Duck), p. 138
P.O. Box 140
Penngrove 94951
(707) 795-3797

Willie Bird Turkeys, p. 139
5350 Highway 12
Santa Rosa 95407
(707) 545-2832

Willowside Meats
3421 Guerneville Rd.
Santa Rosa 95401
(707) 546-8404

FARMS (PRODUCE)

Chester Aaron Garlic, p. 145
P.O. Box 388
Occidental 95465
(707) 874-3114

Crane Melons, p. 41
4947 Petaluma Hill Rd.
Penngrove 94951
(707) 795-6987

DeVoto Gardens
655 Gold Ridge Rd.
Sebastopol 95472
(707) 823-6650

Dry Creek Peach and Produce
2179 Yoakim Bridge Rd.
Healdsburg 95448
(707) 433-7016

Gourmet Mushrooms, p. 145
P.O. Box 391
Sebastopol 95472
(707) 823-1743
gourmetmushroomsinc.com

Hector's Bees, p. 86
2794 Fulton Rd.
Santa Rosa 95403
(707) 579-9416

Kozlowski Farms, p. 168
5566 Gravenstein Hwy.
Forestville 95436
(707) 887-1587
kozlowskifarms.com

Middleton Farm, p. 186
2651 Westside Rd.
Healdsburg 95448
(707) 433-4755

Red Barn Store at Oak Hill Farm
15101 Sonoma Hwy
Glen Ellen 95442
(707) 996-6643

Tierra Vegetables
13684 Chalk Hill Rd.
Healdsburg 95448
(707) 837-8366
tierravegetables.com

Westside Farms
7097 Westside Rd.
Healdsburg 95488
(707) 431-1432

FISH/SEAFOOD

Hog Island Oyster Co., p. 64
P.O. Box 829
Marshall 94940
(707) 663-9218
hogislandoysters.com

Lucas Wharf
595 Highway 1
Bodega 94922
(707) 875-3571

The Tides Wharf Fresh Fish Market
835 Highway 1
Bodega Bay 94922
(707) 875-3554

OLIVE OIL

B.R. Cohn
15140 Sonoma Hwy.
Glen Ellen 95442
(707) 938-4064

McEvoy Ranch
P.O. Box 341, 5935 Redhill Road
Petaluma 94953-0341
(707) 778-2307

The Olive Press
14301 Arnold Dr.
Glen Ellen 95442
(707) 939-8900
theolivepress.com

Toscano-Sonoma (DaVero Extra Virgin
Olive Oil) p. 186
1195 Westside Rd.
Healdsburg 95448
(707) 431-8000
davero.com

RESTAURANTS

Applewood Inn & Restaurant, p. 184
13555 Highway 116
Guerneville 95446
800 555-8509

Della Santina's, p. 78
133 E. Napa St.
Sonoma 95476
(707) 935-0576

Downtown Bakery & Creamery,
p. 118
308A Center St.
Healdsburg 95448
(707) 431-2719

Dry Creek Kitchen, p. 196
25 Matheson St.
Healdsburg 95448
(707) 922-5399

The Duck Club Restaurant,
pp. 41, 166
Bodega Bay Lodge and Spa
103 Highway 1
Bodega Bay 94923
(707) 875-3525

Feast, American Bistro, p. 169
714 Village Court
Santa Rosa 95495
(707) 591-9800

Gary Chu's Gourmet
Chinese Cuisine, p. 139
611 5th St.
Santa Rosa 95404
(707) 526-5840

The General's Daughter Restaurant,
p. 83
400 W. Spain St.
Sonoma 95487
(707) 938-4004

The Girl & the Fig, p. 39
110 W. Spain St.
Sonoma 95487
(707) 938-3634

The Girl & the Gaucho, p. 84
13690 Arnold Dr.
Glen Ellen 95442
(707) 938-2130

Jimtown Store, pp. 86, 194
6706 State Hwy.
Jimtown 95448
(707) 433-1212

John Ash & Co., p. 86
4330 Barnes Rd.
Santa Rosa 95403
(707) 527-7687

Kenwood Inn & Spa, pp. 84–85
10400 Sonoma Hwy.
Kenwood 95452
(800) 353-6966

Lucas Wharf
595 Highway 1
Bodega Bay 94922
(707) 875-3522

Madrona Manor, p. 117
1001 Westside Rd.
Healdsburg 95448
(707) 433-4231

MIXX, pp. 64, 170, 186
135 4th St.
Santa Rosa 95401
(707) 573-1344

Oakville Grocery, p. 195
124 Matheson
Healdsburg 95448
(707) 433-3200

Ristorante Piatti, p. 80
405 1st St. W.
Sonoma 95476
(707) 996-2351

St. Francis Winery Kitchen,
pp. 40, 117, 147
100 Pythian Road
Santa Rosa 95409
(707) 833-4666

Santé Restaurant, p. 80
Sonoma Mission Inn & Spa
18140 Sonoma Hwy.
Boyes Hot Springs 95476
(707) 938-9000

Santi, p. 184
21047 Geyserville Ave.
Geyserville 95441
(707) 857-1790

Sassafras Restaurant, p. 81
1229 Dutton Ave.
Santa Rosa 94507
(707) 578-7600

Swiss Hotel, pp. 78, 138
18 West Spain St.
Sonoma 95476
(707) 938-2884

The Tides Wharf & Restaurant,
p. 170
835 Highway 1
Bodega Bay 94922
(707) 875-3652

Zazu, p. 42
3535 Guerneville Rd.
Santa Rosa 95403
(707) 523-4814

(Recipes from contributors are referenced by page numbers)